1 WEEK 1 THING

1 WEEK
1 THING

FREEDOM AND PEACE FOR THE
BUSINESS OWNER TO ACHIEVE
UNIMAGINABLE BREAKTHROUGHS
IN JUST 4 PAGES A WEEK.

JEFFREY NOTT

NEW DEGREE PRESS

COPYRIGHT © 2019 AUTHOR

1 WEEK 1 THING

Freedom and peace for the business owner to achieve unimaginable breakthroughs in just 3 pages a week.

ISBN   978-1-64137-333-3   *Paperback*

        978-1-64137-646-4   *Ebook*

CONTENTS

INTRODUCTION

———

I wish I had this book when I first started my first business.

I was your typical business owner: good at what I did, I but had no real business knowledge. So how did I make up for my lack of knowledge? Work more hours! My typical day was twelve to fourteen hours and most weeks I worked six days. To the outside observer my business looked very successful because we were always busy. But there were problems that many did not see.

My cashflow was up and down and I didn't understand why I had $50,000 in the bank one month and a negative $20,000 the next. I was so busy and could only wonder, 'Where did the money go?' Employee turnover was high (part of the problem that comes with a business that hires just above minimum wage). I was handling so many tasks that whenever I decided I needed a break and took several days off, business would drop off and productivity plummeted because I did not have any good systems in place.

No one taught me about team building, budgets, labor laws, pricing structures, marketing, or any of the other key items that are essential to having a successful business. My partner was some help and the oil company sent me to dealer training school, but they covered only some of the things I needed to know, and I was still working like crazy.

One definition of a good business that I heard years later: A successful, profitable business is one that works without you.

At the beginning, my business still did not work well without me. I always ended up working more hours in the business (an easy thing for me to do) to make up for the shortfalls. What I didn't do was work on the business. I needed to fix the issues—the hard jobs such as procedures—that would free me from having to work so hard on so many things. Not a great scenario.

"Do the hard jobs first. The easy jobs will take care of themselves."
—DALE CARNEGIE

Much has been written on doing the hard jobs first thing in the morning, so we do not procrastinate by doing the easy jobs first only to realize at the end of the day that we did not take care of the hard jobs.

As Stephen Covey points out in *The 7 Habits of Highly Successful People*, many of us tend to get caught up in doing the easy jobs and our attention is always called away by the tyranny of the urgent activities, some important, some not. Our attention to the *"Not Urgent but Important"* tasks is overpowered by *"Urgent Important and Not Important"* tasks. [1]

That's where I was—I was taking care of the Urgent instead of the Not Urgent. Part of the problem was that I didn't know what some of the Not Urgent but Important things that I should have been doing. This is where education comes in. Things started to turn around when I started taking more business classes and talking with other business owners.

I remember one of those business owners asking me, *"What is your break-even cost?"*

And I asked, *"What is that?"*

---

1   Stephen Covey, *The 7 Habits of Highly Successful People* (New York: Fireside, 1989) 151.

It was then that I began to track some vital numbers. I had a good business but not a great one. I received some good education that helped, but what I needed was a book like this one to really put me over the top.

In coaching other businesses, I came to realize something about myself and many other business owners: Most of us struggle with the idea of starting with the hard jobs first because of one simple letter.

S.

Hard JobS. Yes, that "S" on the end.

"I am rather like a mosquito in a nudist camp; I know what I want to do, but I don't know where to begin."

—DAVID ALLEN, *GETTING THINGS DONE: THE ART OF STRESS-FREE PRODUCTIVITY*

It's a killer because I was starting with too many jobs in my business and years later, I was asking my coaching clients to do the same.

For me, that moment was one of the few times I'd say, *"Dale Carnegie was wrong."* You do only one hard job first. One at a time.

✶✶

Henry is your typical small business owner, much like I was when I started out.

He started his business because he had a keen interest in something. He liked cars and was good at fixing them, so he bought himself an auto repair shop and did what most business owners do: He opened the doors and just started working. And like most small business owners, he struggled to complete the hard jobs such as making an employee manual, writing up job descriptions, or drawing up a simple organizational chart.

When it came time to hire a new manager, he failed with multiple new hires. In the words of the book E-Myth, he abdicated his accountability as an owner[2] by allowing the new hire to run the business without proper orientation because he chose not to do the hard things ahead of time. Like most business owners, it was easier to take care of the urgent issues he faced each day.

He needed some help and brought me in to assess things.

---

2   Michael Gerber, *The E-Myth Revisited* (New York: HarperCollins, 2010), 61.

He was like a lot of my clients when we first met—he was starting with the hard things. But much like me, he had a similar blind spot.

That S.

The result was that he did not make the money he wanted and was frustrated by how his business was operating.

SOBERING STATISTICS

According to SBA statistics, 99.9 percent of all businesses in the USA are considered small, having five hundred or fewer employees.[3] About 85 percent have twenty or fewer employees. And a most disturbing statistic is that only about 50 percent of all these businesses will still exist five years from now.[4] Payscale reports in 2018, the median salary of small business owner/operators was $58,958,[5] not that much higher than the average income of an employee, which was approximately $50,000. [6]Where are you in comparison to the average business owner? And how many hours do you work in comparison to a regular employee?

---

3   2019 Small Business Profile https://bit.ly/2VOWcUZ
4   2012 Small Business Facts https://bit.ly/2J2OP5Y
5   2019 Payscale https://bit.ly/2qfGh6b
6   2018 Social Security Administration https://bit.ly/2cwxEMq

This book is designed to help you exceed that SBA average business owner's income and stay in business for many more years. It is your guide through a process of getting to a new and unimaginable level of success and going through the process repeatedly until your reach the goals you desired when you first started your business.

In this book we will learn from other people's business experiences, including:

- Larry, who learned how to work on his business and found a way to dedicate the time to do so.
- Bruce, who helped a company's team come together to help each other through team meetings.
- Bob, whose company is all about giving back to the community, which has led to greater employee morale and a deeper sense of purpose.
- Paulo, the printer who increased his average sale with a simple list.
- Ravinder, who has increased his employee retention through having team goals.

NOT ANOTHER BUSINESS BOOK

There are tons of books out there about improving your business, being a better manager, learning how to lead, and more

- Entrepreneurs: those that may have many outlets, divisions, or businesses to work with.
- Medium-sized businesses: those with many teams and levels to deal with.
- "*Solo-preneurs*": most of the book will apply, but team chapters not so much. (Might write a book just for these folks.)

THE WAY I SEE IT

The chapters are laid out as they are on purpose. The first few chapters are put first because they cover the most important parts of a business— "*The Big Rocks*" (see story below). Several chapters are designed to follow each other. Many will reference other chapters. But you are free to jump in wherever you feel you need to start (see the next chapter about putting out a fire). You are on your own to wander these pages (I won't be looking over your shoulder), but you should make it a goal to complete every chapter within a year. This way you will have covered just about every part of your business in detail.

You might find that some of the chapters are very similar to others you may have read earlier. Several are, but they are written with a different focus and are broken up in this way so you can complete the assignment in one week. For instance, marketing is the topic in at least three chapters—it needs to be broken up.

YOU MUST START WITH THE BIG THINGS

In the book *First Things First*, Stephen Covey shares the following story, which reflects the basis of my book:[7]

"One day, a time management expert was speaking to a group of business students and, to drive home a point, used an illustration those students will never forget.

As this man stood in front of the group of high-powered over-achievers, he said, *"Okay, time for a quiz."* Then, he pulled out a one-gallon, wide-mouthed Mason jar and set it on a table in front of him. Then he produced about a dozen fist-sized rocks and carefully placed them, one at a time, into the jar.

When the jar was filled to the top and no more rocks would fit inside, he asked, *"Is this jar full?"*

Everyone in the class said, *"Yes."*

Then he said, *"Really?"* He reached under the table and pulled out a bucket of gravel. Then he dumped some gravel in and

---

7   Stephen Covey, A. Roger Merrill, Rebecca Merrill, *First Things First* (New Your: Simon & Schuster, 1994) 88-89

shook the jar, causing pieces of gravel to work themselves down into the spaces between the big rocks.

Then, he asked the group once more, *"Is the jar full?"*

By this time, the class was onto him. *"Probably not,"* one of them answered.

"Good!" he replied. He reached under the table and brought out a bucket of sand. He started dumping the sand in and it went into all the spaces left between the rocks and the gravel.

Once more he asked the question, *"Is this jar full?"*

"No!" the class shouted.

Once again, he said, *"Good!"* Then, he grabbed a pitcher of water and began to pour it in until the jar was filled to the brim.

Then, he looked up at the class and asked, *"What is the point of this illustration?"*

One eager beaver raised his hand and said, *"The point is, no matter how full your schedule is, if you try really hard, you can always fit some more things into it!"*

"*No,*" the speaker replied, "*that's not the point. The truth this illustration teaches us is: If you don't put the big rocks in first, you'll never get them in at all.*"

The main idea of this book is that each week you focus on one important area (the big rocks) of your business. As you progress through the book, the assignments will still be important, but they will be the smaller parts that fill your jar.

For example, it is much easier to work on your marketing when you know what is your "*Why*" and what are your values.

CHANGE IS INEVITABLE.

This book is something you can use year after year. You will need to adapt as your business grows and the business environment changes. So be prepared to start the book over every year.

As you grow, so will your view of your business. Maybe you want to expand, change the focus of the business, or start planning for a sale or transfer the business. Someday you will want to retire. This book can help.

CHAPTER 1

PUT THE FIRE OUT.

———

Jim was really good at what he did: overhauling transmissions and repairing cars. But he had a big problem: He was struggling to make enough money to pay the mortgage payments on time for the building that housed his repair shop. He bought the building five years earlier and was initially doing well, but as the economy tanked during the Great Recession, the business was not making as much money as before. The irregular (often late!) mortgage payments resulted in the bank calling the full payment of the note every few months. He would get caught up but then start to fall behind, and the cycle continued. The stress was killing him. He had a good business and very loyal customers, but he could not figure out what to do.

So, he hired me as his business coach.

I looked over the business and determined that the first thing to do was raise his rates. Jim had not raised his rates since the move to the new building and, even then, he was well below the market. So, he raised his rates by only $10 per hour. One week went by and no one complained or even noticed. Then, he raised his rates another $10 per hour and the same thing happened: no complaints. So, he raised his rates another $10. Still no complaints. Jim's rate was still below the going local market rates, but his cash flow increased immensely. He was now able to pay his bills on time and thereby eliminate the stress of the bank notices.

IS YOUR HOUSE ON FIRE?

When planning what is important, we must, at times, consider the urgent needs of our business before we address other important needs. When the house is on fire, we can't focus on the weeds in the garden, the roof that needs maintenance, or the leaky faucet in the kitchen. Only after the fire is out, can we go back and address the regular maintenance of the home and any additions or renovations we wish to make.

The same goes for one's business.

Once Jim was making his regular payments to the bank, he mind was freed up to be able to focus on the other needs of his business, such as hiring more staff and developing other processes to enhance the operation of his business.

AN ALTERNATIVE WAY TO USE THIS BOOK

As mentioned in the previous chapter, the book is laid out to cover one's business needs in a purposeful order. But if you have a fire to put out, feel free to take a direct dive into that chapter which will help you with the fire you are currently fighting.

If you are having team issues, visit the *"Team"* chapters

If you need more customers, visit the *"Marketing"* chapters

If you are dealing with profitability, visit the *"Know Your Numbers," "Increase Your Average Sale,"* or *"Productivity"* chapters

If you are having issues with conversion rates (closing the sale), visit the *"Talk Guidelines"* chapters.

If these don't fit your needs, each chapter comes with a title that should help you to understand its focus and makes it easy to choose the appropriate one for you.

Figuring out your *"Why"* may seem inconsequential, but it helps in many ways when you want to expand your business, hire employees, and get through the bad days when you feel like giving up. Knowing your Why is vital for both your customers and employees to understand your business. It helps you in making future business decisions more easily when your Why is clear, for example, when developing and building your marketing messaging.

Believe it or not, you already have a Why. You started your business with it in mind, but perhaps you never formalized it into a statement. This exercise can be challenging and can take a bit of time, but it will be well worth it. Remember it is not what you do (write wills, build houses, make meals, etc.) or how you do it, but why you do it.

Here are some questions that can help you determine your Why:

- Why do your customers come to you instead of the competition? Is there something you or your business is best at or known for?
- Why did you start your business? Most get into business because they were good at what they do or had an affinity for something. But what was the problem you wanted to solve or service area that you saw lacking? That is the *"Why."*

- What is the outcome of what you do for your customers? How does that affect their lives?
- What changes do you hope to make in your industry/community/world?
- What are you passionate about?
- What gets you excited about what you do and could be a rallying call for your team?

Maybe you are in the restaurant business. Your *"Why"* could be to provide a great dining experience or create extraordinary meals that will be remembered.

A home improvement company might say, 'We build comfortable living spaces that last.'

Creating a Why statement is like the melding of a Mission and a Vision Statement. Your WHY Statement should be simple, clear, actionable, and focused on how you'll help others. Here are some examples of good Why statements:

- Nordstrom's Mission: To give customers the most compelling shopping experience possible.
- Alzheimer's Association Vision: A world without Alzheimer's disease
- My wife's Why (she is a school nurse): I want the children to be happy, healthy, and ready to learn.

Take the time to ask your team for ideas and thoughts. They may have some great insights you might not have considered.

Many businesses add to their Why Statement a set of Values. You could start this assignment with this list first as it might help you to build your Why Statement. These statements can be anything from just one word like *"integrity"* or *"quality"* to a full sentence like *"Focus on the user and all else will follow."* You should end up with five, and up to a maximum of ten, values.

There are many great tools available online to help you with this week's task. The first is to view this TED Talk by Simon Sinek. It is about eighteen minutes long. Be sure to take some notes.

Here is the link to the video: https://bit.ly/1fJPwPe

To see a list of several company's core values, go to these sites:

https://bit.ly/2twmsWf

https://bit.ly/2OwQXJ5

https://bit.ly/2VUHXhs

The goal here is to come up with at least a few words and/or statements to get things started. You will come up with others as you go about your business and will want to revisit and review this on an annual basis. Zappos had taken some time to develop their list of values—they asked every employee for feedback prior to completing the list![8] Your Why may never change but your values might. The market (and possibly your business focus) changes. People and society change and grow. So be a bit flexible with your values.

In the book *Good to Great*, the author introduces the *"three circles of the hedgehog"* concept.[9] I list the basics of it here because it aligns somewhat with Sinek's *"Golden Circle"* and may be of help in illustrating the concept of Why.

The questions that identify the three circles of the hedgehog concept:

1. What you are deeply PASSIONATE ABOUT (Why)

2. What drives your ECONOMIC ENGINE (What)

3. What you CAN BE THE BEST IN THE WORLD AT (How)

---

8   Tony Hsieh, *Delivering Happiness* (New York: Hachett Book Group, 2010) 154-160

9   Jim Collins, *Good to Great* - Concepts (2019) https://bit.ly/2KDjqrc

We will cover the hedgehog concept in more detail in Week 26: What are you best at.

A quick word about Mission and Vision Statements: You don't have to make them, unless you really feel the need to do so and have lots of time to build them. Why and Value statements are much more powerful, quicker to come up with, and more understandable and actionable by your team and customers. Building Mission/Vision statements are a low priority with many of the coaches and consultants I know and work with.

Your assignment this week:

- Review some of the links listed in this chapter
- Answer the list of questions to determine your Why (add your own as needed)
- Meet with your team (your spouse/partner can/should be included) to ask for suggestions
- Come up with a simple Why statement
- Make a list of values—keep it simple and just start it.
- Revisit this exercise annually

Once you have these formalized, you will have a great foundation to drive you to bigger and better things in so many areas of your business.

See you next week. Wait 'til you see what's on the calendar!

CHAPTER 2

WEEK 2—DEFAULT CALENDAR: THE SECRET TO MAKING THIS BOOK REALLY WORK FOR YOU.

———

"You may delay, but time will not."

—*BENJAMIN FRANKLIN*

Benjamin Franklin had a simple set schedule for his life. He scheduled his sleep time, start of the day rituals, work hours, and more. By doing so, the man accomplished a lot in his life.

He was well read, is broadly quoted, was a statesman, and a prodigious inventor.

The morning question, What good shall I do this day?	5	Rise, wash, and address *Powerful Goodness* ; contrive day's business and take the resolution of the day; prosecute the present study; and breakfast.
	6	
	7	
	8	
	9	Work.
	10	
	11	
	12	Read or overlook my accounts, and dine.
	1	
	2	
	3	Work.
	4	
	5	
	6	
	7	Put things in their places, supper, music, or diversion, or conversation; examination of the day.
	8	
Evening question, What good have I done today?	9	
	10	
	11	
	12	
	1	Sleep.
	2	
	3	
	4	

[10]

To make the main idea of this book, 1 Week 1 Thing, work for you, you should set up your own default calendar and set a time to work on the 1 Thing throughout the week. Working on the topic of each week should take anywhere from one to three hours to launch, review, develop, and/or implement. It should take you fifteen to thirty minutes of your time each

10   Aly Juma, The 13 Virtues of Life: Benjamin Franklin's Guide to Building Character https://bit.ly/2pA5B6v

day to complete. As you complete the task, there will be some details to work on in future weeks, but they will become part of your regular routine. The goal, as stated in my introduction, is to get the Big Things that have been on your list or never were on your list (for too long) started, completed or updated each week.

TIME CHUNKING

Gary Keller, in his book *The One Thing*, talks about *"time chunking."* Keller has made it clear that productivity is the driving force behind your success. As Keller explains, *"Go to your calendar and block off all the time you need to accomplish your ONE Thing. Everything else—other projects, paperwork, e-mail, calls, correspondence, meetings, and all the other stuff—must wait."* You must physically block off the time(s) you want to dedicate to your ONE thing. And do it every single day as you want this to become an established habit. 11

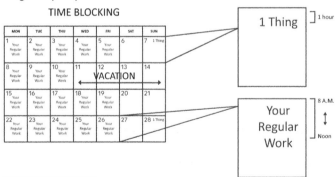

---

11   Gary Keller, Jay Papasan, *The One Thing* (Relleck Publishing Partners, 2013)

Keller really believes in time blocking as the key to scheduling your work. By making an appointment to work on your ONE thing, you are making a commitment to yourself and your future.

"Great success shows up when time is devoted every day to becoming great."

—GARY KELLER

Psychologists Brian Galla and Angela Duckworth in *The Power of Self Control* say structuring your life is a skill. People who do the same activity—like running or meditating—at the same time each day have an easier time accomplishing their goals. Not because of their willpower, but because the routine makes it easier. 12It takes time trying to decide what to do and sometimes we don't do anything because we are frozen in our decision making. Routines free you to do more with the things that matter.

PICK A PROGRAM

There are multiple time management programs out there. This is the week to review and choose which will work for you. Some prefer a basic planner like a Franklin Covey program,

---

12   Brian Galla, Angela Duckworth. Why Willpower is Overrated (Blog: Vox, 2018) https://bit.ly/2FUEXsY

and some would rather use the calendar on their phone and/ or PC. Or, you can just start with the Simple Default Calendar (get a copy at www.1week1thing.com/default calendar). The sample calendar is a guide for you to use to get started. Begin by adding the main things you must do each day (work with clients, reports, emails, work on this book, etc.) and then fill in the things you want to do. It doesn't have to be perfect. You can adjust as you go. Once you complete this book, you will find the need to review this anew as your life will have changed considerably.

Your assignments for this week:

- Determine which calendar/planning program you want to work with
- Block out the time for working on the weekly projects of this book
- Fill out the rest of your schedule—this should include recreation, exercise, and other essential activities
- Visit www.1week1thing.com for more time management suggestions
- Revisit this chapter annually, as your time needs (and desires) will change

Another link you should put on your calendar to review: https://bit.ly/2mtnLFF

Mark a time in your calendar to read this book, otherwise you might miss the next chapter on Goals!!

CHAPTER 4

WEEK 3—GOALS/ BUSINESS PLAN: A MAP TO KNOW WHERE YOU WANT TO GO AND WHEN YOU HAVE ARRIVED

———

You already know that frightening statistic of 85 percent of all businesses will fail in their first 5 years is a lie.

I'll repeat the good news: according to the SBA, the real number is much lower at around 50 percent. While this number is considerably easier to stomach, no one wants to be one of the losing 50 percenters!

Why do so many fail?

The lack of a good plan.

BEGIN WITH THE END IN MIND

"Begin with the end in mind" is one of my favorites of Stephen Covey's *7 Habits of Highly Successful People."*

13

How do most business owners start a business? They usually start with a dream, a skill they possess and/or a strong desire to control their own destiny. The owner may be great in the avocation they have chosen or have a hot new idea, widget or app, but they have little or no education on what it takes to run the business side of things. They start out by hanging their shingle over the front door (or building a website) and wait for the clients to roll in. Some may be lucky in the first year of opening as friends and family usually support them, but as time goes by, the lack of a plan begins to take its toll. Typically, most businesses start to feel the strains of this lack of a plan in the third and fourth year, and by the fifth year,

---

13   Covey, *The 7 Habits of Highly Successful People*, 95-144

they close the doors due to burnout and lack of cash. They go back to work for someone else making more money as an employee. Remember the statistics in the introduction? The average business owner makes a paltry $8958 a year more than most employees. Or, they try to start another business with some new idea or product only to end up closing that business in a few years as well.

There are five areas that are considered the main causes of business failure:

- Cashflow—lack of profits and/or sales, excessive costs
- Marketing—poorly written plan or none at all, wrong target, low budget
- Management skills— no budgets, inventory control, capital management
- Team management/recruitment— no set methods to get and keep good employees
- Lack of systems—how everything doesn't get done day-to-day

WHAT'S YOUR PLAN?

This book is not intended to be used for starting a new business, though it could be; it is designed to be used by an existing business owner to get on track, with one major thing each week. But since many businesses never make a decent business plan, the focus this week is to make up a simple plan as a guide going forward. Or maybe you did make up a plan, but now it's time to review that plan and modify as needed. In the process of doing business, many things change—the market, the products/services, the culture and the owner's lives.

In Week 1, the *"Why"* chapter, we discussed the reasons WHY you do WHAT you do. In this chapter, we lay out your goals and the HOW for the business.

YOUR TRAVEL PLANS

Imagine this plan as if you were making up a travel itinerary. Would you show up to the airport one day to buy a ticket to someplace that you just decided that day you wanted to visit? Of course, not (unless you are independently wealthy!). There is a lot to plan if you want to have a good trip. Where do you want to go? How much will it cost to get there? What will be the day to day costs? Who do you want to take with you? What sights do you want to see? How will you get there and back? How long will you be away? Who will take care of the business, the pets, the house, the bills and all the other things you would normally do?

The first step is to answer a few questions that will assist you in figuring out how to make this plan.

- Why did you start this business? There must be some motivating factor, such as, *"I was good at _____,"* or *"I wanted to help_____."* (You should have this answer from chapter 3)
- How much money do you want or need to make? You need to have a target to work on budgets, etc.
- How much time do you want to work in and on the business? It must be realistic in the effort you are willing to put in.
- How big do you want it to be? Whatever you want is OK. Things may change later, but you need to have an idea to remain focused.
- What do you want your position to be in the business? Do you want to be CEO or just a worker? (Discussed in detail in Week 12 – Do you know your role?)
- How many employees do you need? And what does the organizational chart look like? You need to know who will be needed, where, and what their duties will be.
- What is the budget for the operations? You must know how much money you need to just run the place. (This just happens to be covered in Week 5).
- What is the end game for the business? Do you want to sell it, leave it for family or just make the most money until you can't operate it anymore?

The answers to these questions will help you determine your goals and make a good plan. Reviewing your plan and these questions on an annual basis is important to do as change is the one constant of the universe. It is okay to change your goals as you go through life. It's just like you deciding to stay an extra day on your planned trip because you discovered some quaint village you want to explore.

If you want to make up a more formal business plan you can get a free template, offered by SCORE, at this link: https://bit.ly/2m23yGI

Your assignment this week:

- Answer the questions listed. Don't spend hours doing so, just jot down the first few things that pop into your mind.
- Got to www.1week1thing for forms and tables and additional questions that will help you with this 1 Thing. Using these forms will speed up the process and not take weeks to come up with some simple goals and plans.
- Review your plans and goals and budget annually (at least) to make sure you are on track.
- One goal that must be in the plan—to finish this book!

Once you have your plan completed you should have it reviewed by your mentor or business coach for feedback. Or, if you use the SCORE template, you can take it to a local SCORE coach for review for at no charge.

See you next week—it's all about the numbers!

CHAPTER 5

WEEK 4—KNOW YOUR NUMBERS: DIGGING IN

———

"'Know your numbers' is a fundamental precept of business."

—BILL GATES

To be honest, I did not know any of the important numbers when I owned my first business. All I knew was an approximate total dollar of sales I was shooting for each month with an ongoing goal to do more the next month. I was just like many business owners, where I focused on the money in the bank and, if it was too low, find a way to work harder (which meant more hours) and sell more services. It usually worked, but it's not the best way to live!

The only numbers I usually worked on, other than the monthly total, came from my bookkeeper. About fifteen to twenty days after the end of each month he would review my reports with me and tell me where I needed to improve my sales and margins or reduce some costs. Imagine how much money I lost because I did not get my bad news until many days into the new month! No one ever told me about Key Performance Indicators (known as KPIs—see the list below) and why I should know them. If I had known what they were and tracked them daily, I could have done so much better (made more money!) and worked a lot fewer crazy hours. This is not any way to run a business, especially if one ever wanted to sell the business someday for a tidy sum.

Today I know so much more as a result of my many hours of business education from workshops, webinars, and reading books and industry periodicals. I encourage you to look into the various forms of business education, if you haven't already done so in Week 42.

"What gets measured gets done."

—PETER DRUCKER

What KPIs do you need to know? The basics are the same for almost all businesses, but many have specifics they should be tracking. The basics that you should know for any type of business are the costs of running your business on an hourly, daily and monthly basis, your breakeven sales total, and your gross profit percentage to achieve your desired net profit percentage.

Here are some KPIs that I look for when working with a client:

- Average Sale Amount—per transaction, compare with industry averages.
- Number of Sales/Invoices—per day, week, month.
- Conversion rate—number of calls/prospects to closed sales.
- Inventory turn—what is selling well or not. (Covered in more detail in Week 40.)
- Average Sales per Customer—how can you improve this number?
- Average Lifetime Sale per Customer—know who your best customers are.
- Employee Productivity and Efficiency—are the hours worked fully utilized.
- Gross Profit Margin—the profit on sales before the fixed costs are paid.
- Net Profit Margin—what the business keeps after paying all the bills.
- Sales/profits per category—to determine what to keep selling or improve on.

- Average Sales this month versus one year ago – how are you doing real time
- Breakeven cost—how much does it cost just to keep the doors open and the bills paid?

There are many more numbers one can track. Here are two links that list more for you to consider:

https://bit.ly/2MMUiAa

https://bit.ly/2qXa3XY (not an endorsement of their product, but an extensive list and a possible solution to help you do the tracking of your KPIs.)

What you need to do is figure out what KPIs you should be tracking for your business. Reach out to your bookkeeper/accountant, peers in your industry, a coach or consultant, or do some research online on how to get those numbers. You should be able to get them from a bookkeeping or point of sale program. There are many programs available for every industry and I encourage you to investigate the options rather than using something generic like Quickbooks or Peachtree. This task may take more than one week to complete all that you want or need to track. But getting a start on the most important KPIs will make a huge difference in the operation and profitability of your business. You will feel more empowered when you start to know your numbers.

Your assignment this week:

- Figure out what KPIs you should be tracking (if you don't know them already)
- Ask your bookkeeper and your peers for suggestions on what to track
- Look for industry standards to compare with your numbers (online or in industry publications)
- Seek an industry coach or trainer for assistance in tracking and understanding the numbers
- Set up regular reporting (daily, weekly, monthly) to keep on top of your numbers

You will want to review these numbers every year as you plan the next year's budget and goals.

I count on seeing you next week when we discuss Marketing.

CHAPTER 6

WEEK 5—MARKETING: TARGET AND GOALS

———

"You can't hit a target if you don't know what it is."

—ANTHONY ROBBINS

I spoke with marketing man Dave Parkhurst of GreenHaven Interactive about what he sees as real challenges for him in working with many businesses for the first time. *"The two biggest challenges I have is the owner does not have a budget for marketing nor a well-defined target market! They do what I call 'ad hoc marketing' which is going with whatever marketing sales rep approaches them with some great deal promising to get more customers."* It basically comes down to not having a targeted market and a budget.

Let's start with the easy part: how to determine what your marketing budget should be. Most accountants, consultants and honest marketers will tell you that a budget of 4 to 8 percent of your total gross revenue is the figure you should use.

Another good tip: you should always be marketing! If business is doing very well, you can back off some to the 4 percent level, but if business is not doing well you need to spend more. Many businesses cut back their marketing in bad times to save money, but that is the worst thing one could do.

WHAT IS MARKETING?

Marketing is not sales. What constitutes marketing is anything you do to promote your business to prospects, your current customers and your business partners (those that refer business to you). This would be items like your customer follow-up and appreciation programs, kids' sports teams' sponsorships, Chamber membership, website, social media, publications, advertisements, promotional items, window signs, thank you gifts, discount coupons, and more. Quite a range, but they all count in your marketing budget. If you know what your budget is, you know how much you can spend, thereby helping you to know your return on Investment. And a good budget will keep you from buying any *"ad hoc"* deals.

GOTTA HAVE A TARGET

Now for the less easy part of marketing: your target market. Do you know who your target market is? Can you give a good description of what your ideal client looks like? I often tell the story of the salon owner, who, when asked, *"Who is your target market?"* responded *"Anyone with hair!"* Well, that sounds like a great target if you are willing to service everyone in your area, but how do you market to all those people? What one or two messages can you use to get them into your business? It becomes a lot more complicated.

To simplify you marketing efforts, make a list of what your ideal client looks like. Using the salon for example, the woman said her preferred customer was a thirty-five- to fifty-five-year-old woman, upper middle to lower upper class, drove a luxury car such as a Cadillac, BMW, Lexus, Audi, or Mercedes, ate at the nicer restaurants in the area, read magazines like Architectural Digest and Travel + Leisure, went to the theater often, and volunteered at a number of nonprofits. That is a pretty specific target, don't you think? We know a lot about the prospect, so we should be able to find many specific places to advertise and send the right message (offer). That's a lot easier than advertising to all different demographics just to get some business!

Your assignment for this week:

- Determine who your ideal customer is (or review what you have already).
- Determine how much you are currently spending on marketing (over or under budget?) and adjust.
- Review you current marketing to see if it appeals to your target market.
- Check with your staff for feedback on target market and/ or marketing.

This should be a fun exercise for you: Imagine how much better your business will be when all your clients are your ideal client! If you happen to attract the wrong client—and that will happen—that will be addressed in Week 48.

See you next week when we talk about HR.

CHAPTER 7

WEEK 6—HR POLICIES AND PROCEDURES

"The trend towards throwing new laws at everything continues apace."

—JOHN GARDNER

I was working with a restaurant owner who was having some challenges with an employee he was dismissing. The employee was citing the newly passed California sick leave law and felt that the employer owed him unused sick days. While he was not completely correct on what the law afforded him, he knew more about it than did the owner! If the owner had his HR manual/handbook up to date and an

HR professional to consult with, the issue would have been resolved quickly.

ALWAYS SOMETHING NEW

State, local, and national legislatures pass a seemingly endless list of new rules and regulations every year. The laws are written to protect the employee, but the employer can find help to protect themselves. Employers must educate themselves on these laws, present them to their employees, and implement them fairly and consistently to avoid lawsuits or legal action by the governing authorities. Every January there are labor law update seminars offered in my area by several law firms or hosted by the local Chambers of Commerce that are great sources for information on the new laws. You should look for the same in your area and plan on attending whenever they are held.

Another example of a new law in California: Effective January 1, 2021, all employers with five or more employees will be required to provide two hours of sexual harassment training to supervisors and one hour to non-supervisory employees within six months of hire and every two years after that[14]. (There is more to this law—see your HR professional for more information if you are in California). The law was modified

---

14   RPNA Law Group New California Sexual Harassment Training Requirements 2019 https://bit.ly/31q9HLZ

from the previous fifty-employee company requirement to include companies with as few as five employees. This is a major change that has affected thousands of small businesses in California and may come to other states someday.

GET IT DONE—NOW!

Do you have an HR policies and procedures book? If so, when was the last time it was updated? If you don't have one, then make it a priority to get some HR help ASAP. Even if you are not in California or New York, two of the states with the most onerous of laws, you need to have an HR policies and procedures book (different from an employee handbook—that's for next week). You might ask, 'Why do I need one? I have never had a problem. All my employees love me!' You probably have said the same thing about your clients, but there is always that one that has threatened to sue or has even done so. All it takes is one! And with the complexities of the laws, it is easier than ever to be out of compliance. Many of your employees know enough about the laws, like the one in the story above, that they might challenge you on any one of them.

Your HR policies and procedures would include all the policies required by law, including pay periods, time off, non-discrimination, conduct, and more.

Some places to start the process

If you don't already have a source for your HR needs, here are some places to investigate:

- Your payroll company—many offer some boilerplate handbooks and offer some services to review your edited handbook.
- Your on-call legal service such as LegalShield or other employment attorney may be of help.
- Your local Chamber of Commerce—offers some services, may be able to recommend a HR professional from a list of its members or may have legal resources online.
- Your attorney, banker and/or accountant may have some referrals for you.
- Look into some local networking groups like BNI. They can be found online where many of these groups' members' profiles may be posted for you to review them.
- Do an online search for *"HR manual"* and you will find many templates you can start with before seeing a HR professional to review and update yours.

Once you have found a good HR professional, make it a point to see them on an annual or semi-annual basis. Your manual will need to be updated to reflect any new changes to the laws or benefits you provide. You want to have that HR professional's or a labor law attorney's number handy for whenever you are about to dismiss or discipline an employee. A bad dismissal can have you embroiled in a lawsuit or a visit from the labor commissioner's office.

CAUTION!

We all know there are a lot of resources available on the internet. I will venture a guess that you, and your employees, have already been there for many things. There is a lot of great information available, but there is also a lot of bad information, as well. That wrong information can cost you. That is why you should seek out a professional to review all your policies and procedures.

Your assignment this week:

- Get your HR policies and procedures made up or updated to reflect new laws.
- Seek out an HR professional to engage with.
- Make sure every employee has a copy of the policies and procedures, understands them, and signs a form acknowledging receipt thereof.
- Schedule an annual, or semi-annual, review appointment with your HR professional.

Dealing with an HR manual is not fun (unless you are an HR professional), but there will be a day when you will be happy you did.

Required legal notice: I am not an HR professional nor attorney. The information provided here is for reference only. Please seek professional advice in reviewing and/or implementing any policies.

See you next week when we talk about more employee communications.

CHAPTER 8

WEEK 7—EMPLOYEE HANDBOOK: YOUR BUSINESS GUIDE FOR YOUR TEAM

———

"I favor weapons of mass instruction."

— MICHAEL RAY SMITH, *7 DAYS TO A BYLINE THAT PAYS*

Shirley was looking for a job much closer to home and at a smaller operation. The owner had been looking for a new manager for many months when she applied. Shirley went through the few stages of interviewing, including one with myself and a fellow coach. We felt she was more than qualified but forewarned the owner that she would need a thorough on-boarding and hand-holding during her first few weeks. She was a strong-willed individual and would need some good training to orient her to the slower-paced business. She was given an offer which she happily accepted and was very anxious to start. This was all well and good until the day she started.

On her first day, her employer was called away for two weeks to take care of one of his other businesses and the person that she was destined to replace just happened to be on vacation that week. All she had to work from was the job description from the ad she answered and her experience in the industry. She was not given any orientation, HR manual, or an employee handbook of any kind. Nor was she was properly introduced to the other employees. The team now had to work together with no real instructions or guidance. What are the odds of her being successful in this new place? Slim to none. She lasted three weeks and the business almost lost another employee due to the strife she initially created.

This may seem like something crazy, but I have seen this happen to many Shirleys in other similar scenarios, many times over. The results are usually worse, not to mention all the lost sales and production time. The owner must start the process of looking for a new hire all over again which is typically a six- to eight-week process. (See Week 29 *"Hiring Process"*). This could have been avoided by better on-boarding of the new employee.

A WARM WELCOME

As I sat in my office writing this book, I could hear the cheers and clapping for the new freshmen arriving at a private high school less than a block away. This tradition of sophomores, juniors, and seniors greeting their new classmates in such a joyous way has been going on for many years. I just can't help but wonder how it makes the new students feel on their first day of orientation. And I wonder why more businesses won't do something like this when a new employee arrives on their first day on the job.

Your process doesn't have to start with all the cheering as they walk in the door for the first time (but why not?). It should start with a full review of the employee handbook and HR policy manual, a tour of the offices/facility, and a formal introduction to your team. If you are a retail business, it would be a good idea for each employee to get a name badge and business cards (even if they are just a clean-up person— give them a title like Maintenance Supervisor). Another idea that worked for a call center to retain employees longer: get each new employee a shirt with their name embroidered on it. These ideas may not apply to your business, but the goal here is for you to make the new hire feel special and part of the team as quickly as possible.

SET THE EXPECTATIONS

An employee handbook is not a HR policies and procedures manual, it is a companion to it. The employee handbook contains things like:

- Mission/Vision/Values/Why statements, a welcome statement
- Performance expectations and reviews
- Use of company facilities and company-issued tools and equipment
- Procedures, organizational structure, duties of employees, and what is expected of them.
- A company organizational chart is a nice touch, so all know who is in which department and more

This should be updated about the same time as the HR policies and procedures manual as the change in laws may affect some of your policies.

Some of the benefits of having a well-written employee handbook:

- More satisfied employees who stay longer because they know the 'rules of the road' and what is expected of them
- Reduces the chance of legal actions taken by an employee against the company –
- Improved productivity and teamwork
- Greater customer loyalty due to a consistent level of customer service as all employees are trained in the same manner

Your assignment this week:

- Employee manual—start to build one or review the current manual for any needed changes.
- Have the manual reviewed by an HR professional or attorney for compliance.
- Refer to the *"HR Manual"* chapter for suggested resources to seek out additional help or guidance.
- This exercise should be repeated annually.

There are many online sources of information about this topic (two are listed here). Many offer customizable templates for you to use for free. If you care to do your own searches, it is very important that you look for those sites that are familiar with the laws of your state.

https://bit.ly/2m78qKA   https://bit.ly/2m0vqLw

More exciting exercises await you. See you when we discuss the next week's topic!

CHAPTER 9

WEEK 8—TEAM MEETINGS: THE GLUE THAT BONDS YOUR STAFF

"Coming together is a beginning. Keeping together is progress. Working together is success."

—HENRY FORD

To start off team meetings, the ActionCoach community suggests their clients use what they call the WIFLE. It stands for *"What I Feel Like Expressing."* The idea is for the attendees to share whatever is on their mind, free of any reprisals. Studies show that teams form greater bonds when they feel like they are in a safe environment.

Coach Bruce Wilson shared a story about one of the first team meetings with a client that was quite impactful. The company was a construction firm and, as you can imagine, the employees were made up of blue-collar guys who are not known for being all warm and fuzzy with each other. In the couple of weeks prior to the meeting, the production was off and there was one fellow who was dragging down the whole team. This led to some increased tensions. In the meeting, several voiced their dissatisfaction with the low team productivity and some not pulling their own weight. No one mentioned the man's name, but everyone knew who was being singled out for the issue. When it was finally that man's turn, the first thing he did was apologize for his lack of production and poor attitude. He admitted that he was distracted and stated the cause of the distraction: He found out two weeks earlier that his wife was diagnosed with cancer and her prognosis was not good. Well, that was a bombshell that shook up the team and changed the attitudes immediately. The team became much tighter and all worked to support their coworker.

COMMUNICATION IS VITAL

Do you have regular team meetings where they can share things like the above story? Do you have team meetings at all? Every business should have team meetings on a daily, weekly, monthly, and annual basis. Communication is vital for the owner as well as the team members. Look at any sports team. They not only have a meeting before every game, but many short meetings throughout the game. Your business, no matter how small or big, should consider doing the same.

At the beginning of every day, the team should meet to review the day's activities for fifteen to twenty minutes. Review what may have been left over from the day before, who will be taking on what tasks, what materials/supplies/tools will be needed, who will call who, and many more details. This will lead to increased productivity, less frustration for everyone, and more satisfied customers due to on time delivery of your product or service as everyone has a clear idea of what must be done and by whom. This can be very helpful to the recently hired employee, as well.

Weekly meetings should include a recap of the week and what will be happening in the next meeting. The WIFLE or something similar should be a part of this meeting. The more the team communicates, the better the morale and the better the business will run.

The daily meeting should be no more than twenty minutes and the weekly, depending on the size of your team, should be about thirty minutes.

Monthly meetings would be for reviewing the month's business numbers and discussing goals for the next month and possibly some short education. Celebrate and acknowledge those that have achieved their goals.

Annual meetings should be a less formal affair. Take time to celebrate the accomplishments of the team and a select few standouts. This should be a party. Get them out of the work place to some place they, and you, can relax and enjoy away from the business environment.

People can be one of your biggest liabilities, but they are also your biggest asset. Take time to meet with them to communicate the needs of the business and encourage them to share their needs and suggestions. Show them your appreciation not only in private but in front of their peers, as well. Your company will be much better for it in many ways.

Your assignment for this week:

- Set up daily and weekly meeting agendas. What does your team need to succeed? What is it that you want to share?

- Set up monthly meetings and agendas. These should include a recap of goals achieved for the month (individual, team and company goals).
- Set up an annual meeting and agendas. These should include milestone awards (number of years in service, etc.), as well as personal and company goals achieved, etc.

You will find the more time your team meets, the greater the bond and more productive and happier everyone will be, including you!

Looking forward to more breakthroughs on Procedures in the next week!

CHAPTER 10

WEEK 9—PROCEDURES: BUT WE'VE ALWAYS DONE IT THIS WAY!

"The most dangerous phrase in our language is, 'We've always done it this way.'"

—REAR ADMIRAL GRACE MURRAY HOPPER

The small mom and pop finance company grew very fast during the height of the real estate boom of the early 2000s. They went from just the two founders to over one thousand employees in just a few years. They were processing so many loans that they had a $10,000 high-speed printer that required one full time employee just to keep the machine full of paper! Gregg Fiscalini of Focused Business Solutions was hired by the owners to review their operations to see where he could make some improvements in processes. One day while Gregg was watching the paper processing and talking with the employees involved, an idea was suggested to him by a young intern on the team: why not just use a computer to pull up the documents needed to research the client, thereby avoiding printing altogether? The solution worked, the printer was put to work where they needed it in another office and the paper tender was reassigned.

Where are you losing time and money in your business? We all need to take time out to assess our processes. Two questions were suggested to me by Gregg:

- Why are you doing what you're doing? (Goal)

- How are you doing what you're doing? (Process)

EVERY PROCESS SHOULD BE DOCUMENTED

If you do not have processes and procedures in place (written down), then bad habits can ensue and you get the statement, *"But we have always done it this way!"*

One way to approach this is by writing the most draconian procedures. Present them to your team(s) and let them know what your goals are, the desired target, then let them choose what to do or not to do as long as your goals are achieved. Let the team members have a large amount of control. But let them know that if the targets aren't met, all the draconian procedures will be enforced.

I used to tell my teams, *"I don't really care how you get your work done (the actual procedure). All I want is that the work is done to our standards, done in the time allotted, and keeps the customer happy and coming back."* This process allowed my team to be flexible, which lead many of them to come up with new ways to complete projects in record times while having fun at it.

SO MANY BENEFITS

The advantages of good processes and procedures are myriad. They can lead to fewer accidents (less Workers' Comp claims, absenteeism, etc.), increased productivity, greater teamwork, employee engagement (lower turnover), lower operating costs (less returns, materials, waste, energy use, etc.), scalability of the business, and increased valuation of the business.

Every process and policy should be documented to address not only the day-to-day activities of the business, but to handle the *"When this happens…"* of business before it happens: those events of the unexpected variety. These could be handling an irate customer, doing an exchange or warranty, or learning how to handle an emergency. You want your employees to be able to handle any event. Your goal should be to set things up in your business so well, that it can run just the same (or better) without you being there!

Below is a list of some of the things that should be documented. Feel free to add to it as you see what applies to your business. More can be found at www.1week1thing.com.

- Materials handling—ordering, receiving, stocking, returns, hazardous waste
- Equipment—purchasing, maintenance, depreciation,
- Production—techniques, safety issues, training, clothing,
- Permits & licenses
- Education—continuing education, certification
- Customer service—new customer orientation, follow up, order handling, complaints, delivery of product/services
- Inspections—daily, weekly, monthly, annually—something like fire extinguishers, inventory counts, etc.

Your assignment this week:

- Start listing all the activities of the business
- Start making a procedure/policy to handle each area listed above (or others you deem important).
- Place these in the employee handbook.

- Review these on an annual basis or whenever a new one is needed.

The weekly procedure of working your 1 Thing should already be in your default calendar!

See next week when we talk more marketing..

CHAPTER 11

WEEK 10—REVIEW AND RENEW YOUR MARKETING

"Marketing is like bread: eventually it gets stale, looks bad, and you need a new loaf."

—JEFFREY NOTT

I remember calling on a business owner who was complaining about business being slow. He was on a busy street, but few passersby ever stopped in. I suggested he put some banner flags out to catch the eyes of passersby. He followed my advice and was happy to report that it had boosted his business, for a while. Clearly, they were attractive and caught people's attention, but when I visited him many months later, they had been there so long that they were faded and tattered. Most passersby had gotten visual fatigue and no longer noticed them or, if they did, noticed the shabby shape they were in and probably went someplace else. The rule of thumb is visual materials and displays should be changed up every sixty to ninety days.

GETTING THE RIGHT CLIENT?

Then there was Carlos. He had a busy shop, but he was not making the money he wanted or should have been making. We talked about his marketing and what was working for him. One of his methods was to use the same coupon specials over and over in a local ad mailer that I will call the *"Penny Pincher Paper."* It featured personal as well as business ads. He got a fair amount of business but all the wrong kind—those that always wanted a discount! He was spending $2,000 a month to get $6,000 of business. These numbers looked good until we looked at the reports and found that after the profit margins were applied, he was losing $1,700 every month. We moved that expenditure to another form of advertising that attracted the right clientele, who were a lot more profitable as well as loyal.

What about the marketing pieces you get in your own mail? Ever notice that coupon or flier you have been getting for many months, which still has the same layout, pictures (most likely a stock photo not really representing the business), and *"specials"*? Spaced repetition is good to catch the attention of your prospect, but things need to be changed periodically to keep getting their attention.

TIME TO REVIEW

This is your week to review your marketing and figure out what is stale or maybe needs a different strategy, offer, or target market. The average business will lose 15 to 20 percent of its clientele every year so it's vital that you remain looking for new business. People will move away, find a new place to do their business or die.

But first, let's review a bit about marketing overall (some of which I have covered in other chapters in greater detail):

- Good marketing gets the phone to ring and people to come to your business as well as keeps your current clientele coming back.
- You can't rely on just one thing. A good rule is to have about ten different marketing pieces or campaigns going at the same time.
- Anything with your name on it is marketing.
- You need to test and measure everything—you want to know what's working.

- Expiration date on all your offers every time. This will create urgency and fear of loss—a big motivator for people to take advantage of your offer. Be sure to update or change your offers on any marketing materials that are posted on your website or social media. Everything needs to be refreshed at least quarterly.
- Your marketing budget should 4 to 8 percent of your gross sales. Spend more when you are slow, and less when too busy, but ALWAYS be marketing. No matter what the condition of your business or market, never stop advertising.
- Never advertise a price if you don't have to. Instead offer a bundled package (_____ included with every purchase), a discount if you must (X percent of $X amount of purchase), or a giveaway, such as a restaurant gift card with minimum purchase (see Week 30 *"Mutual Marketing"*). Always promote the value of your product/service, like your guarantee, qualifications, hours, exclusives, etc. One of my clients never advertised price offered discounts— he only talked about the value he gave his customers. He retired recently a very wealthy man.
- Track your marketing to see how well it is doing:
    - By using a distinct phone number for each major piece of marketing (your website should have a different number tracked and calls recorded).
    - Each marketing piece or ad should have a unique offer or promotion.

- Every new client should be asked, *"How did you hear about us?"* They may not remember exactly ('I saw you on the web'), but you should get some idea.
- If any marketing piece is not bringing in clientele or the wrong clientele, cancel it immediately.
- Hire professionals to do all this for you. You stick to what you do and let others do it for you. Yeah, you can do the simple things like Post-Its and pens but leave the other things to them. Many industry groups, your vendors, or Chamber groups are a good place to look for help.

I have more marketing ideas at www.1week1thing.com

Your assignment this week:

- Write down ALL the marketing you are doing: anything that has your name on it.
- Determine how each of these is performing, as best as you can. Review your marketing reports, if you have them. (If you don't have this information, then find a way to start tracking them.)
- Schedule time to delete, update, or add something else to this mix.
- Hire that marketing professional if you have not done so already. Or maybe it's time to review that person?

This exercise should be done on an annual basis, if not more often.

See you next week when we look for some help.

CHAPTER 12

WEEK 11—GET SOME HELP

———

"No matter what accomplishments you make, somebody helps you."

—ALTHEA GIBSON

Larry Moore of Larry's Autoworks went off to an *E-Myth* Training Weekend event where he learned a very important lesson that changed his life: Work on your business, not just in it! To help get him in the frame of a business owner, he decided that he would wear a three-piece suit and a tie. The next thing he did was to set a time every day to work on his business. To help keep him on track, he enlisted the help of his employees. He asked that they do whatever it took to make sure he kept his appointment with himself every day at 2 p.m. This was no easy task as this hour was a busy time in his shop, but it worked for him and he was able to grow a very large and successful business.

If you want to have greater success in whatever you are doing, you need to have some help. This could mean doing something as simple as having your employees hold you accountable like Larry. But there are more ways that can get you better results. You might be missing something that is holding you back from that real breakthrough in your business.

THE "MIRACLE JUMP"[15]

In 1968, Mexico City was then the site of the most shocking leap in long jump history. Both Ralph Boston of the USA and Igor Ter-Ovanesyan of the Soviet Union competed in the 1968 Olympics—the American would earn a bronze medal—but Boston was also mentoring that year's world-leading jumper, fellow American Bob Beamon. After Beamon fouled twice during the qualification round, Boston advised him to move back and start his approach with his opposite foot. Beamon followed the advice and qualified easily. In the final, Beamon shocked everyone—himself included—by soaring more than 21 inches beyond the world record on his first attempt.

---

15   Mike Rosebaum, Men's Long Jump World Records https://bit.
ly/2MPPSZ7 (June 18, 2018)

Disbelieving officials brought out a steel tape measure and double-checked the landing pit before certifying Beamon's distance: 8.90/29-2½. "I didn't go in to break any records," Beamon said later. "I was only interested in winning a gold medal."

Look at any professional athlete, or even the amateurs, and you will see that all of them have a coach. Some athletes have several coaches. Michael Phelps had a coach at his last Olympics even though he had already won many medals at the previous games. Name the sport and all the athletes have coaches. Every athlete knows the power of having a coach. But coaches are not just for sports. There are many different types of coaches, including speech coaches and others that can help us in many areas of our lives.

EVERYONE NEEDS A COACH OR MENTOR

The message here is that every business owner needs to have a coach, mentor, teacher, mastermind group or an accountability partner. Over my lifetime, I have had many of each of these, who have helped me become better at what I was doing. My publisher coached me in the writing of this book. He and his team helped me with more than just how to write the book but encouraged me through some of the rougher times of getting it completed.

There are endless statistics on every industry on how much more money a business will make when the owner has a coach. The International Coach Federation surveyed 210 coaching clients for demographic data and feedback about the value and use of coaching.[16] Some of the statistics on business coaching they gathered are as follows:

70 percent believed business coaching is *"very valuable."*

50 percent confide in their coach as much as their best friend, spouse or therapist

12 percent confide in their coach more than anyone else

Some of the outcomes were:

62.4 percent smarter goal-setting

60.5 percent more balanced life

57.1 percent lower stress levels

52.4 percent more self-confidence

43.3 percent improvement in quality of life

---

16   Coachings Statistics on the Value of Coaching https://bit.ly/35EIHLT (April 15, 2016)

25.7 percent more income

46 percent increase in profit margin

The statistics on business coaching reveal that those who use coaches do improve their chances of success in one way or another. By seeking an external perceptive, you gain the opportunity to receive guidance and advice you may not have ever conceived otherwise. It goes back to earlier chapters where an outside viewpoint helps us to see what we cannot since we can have a *"visual blindness"* to our own environment.

SEEKING A COACH

What to look for in a coach: Does the coach have a good understanding of the basics of business, team building, customer service, marketing, financial spreadsheets, and KPIs? Can they give you some ideas on how to help you attain the goals you have for your business and life? Do you feel like the coach really understands you and is relatable?

There are many places to look for a coach or accountability groups. Start first with your industry association or groups. Ask your fellow business owners to see who they are using. Almost all the best businesses have a coach, mentor, or are part of a business accountability group. You might look to your local Chamber of Commerce for coaches that are members. And you can always search online.

Your assignment this week:

- Seek out some outside help from:
    - another person in your industry that you respect as a mentor.
    - a mastermind group you can join (or start) or some other form of accountability group.
    - a business coach.

You will be amazed at what a good coach or mentor can do for you and your business. And don't forget to share with them your journey through this book.

See you next week when we review your role.

CHAPTER 13

WEEK 12—DO YOU KNOW YOUR ROLE?

———

"Drive thy business or it will drive thee."

—BEN FRANKLIN

Chad Strzegowski and his sister Cara Strzegowski Hierholzer are the third-generation owners of Al's Seafood Restaurant. They took over the business after the passing of their father Albert Louis Strzegowski, Jr. Two years later, they were close to closing the doors of the nearly 60-year-old family business. The finances were in disarray, leadership was nonexistent and there was a divide between the uninspired staff and stubborn management. The business was a disaster. How did this happen and how to fix it?

This scenario was one of the episodes of Restaurant Impossible and it was a real challenge for Robert Irvine, the rescuer of the many restaurants featured on the show[17]. Robert did many different things to right the wrongs in this business, many of which I address throughout this book. The topic highlighted in this chapter is what hit me the hardest while watching this episode play out: the owners did not have set roles for themselves. They were trying to play some roles, but they were in the wrong ones and even then, they didn't stick to them. There were many scenes on the show where Chad would step in and attempt to address an issue and end up frustrating his sister or the employees.

WHAT'S YOUR ROLE?

Of the many business owners I have worked with, too few have had job descriptions for their employees and ever fewer have had a job description for themselves.

When I ask the owner, *"What is your job description?"*

The answer is typically, *"The boss."*

My response: *"Ok, what are you job duties?"*

---

17 Restaurant Impossible The Food Network, First aired August 24, 2019

Their response: *"I run the business and fill in wherever I am needed."*

A very broad description with no detail.

How would an employee handle a job description so broad and unspecific? As the business owner, you need to have a clear-cut description of what you do and what parts of the business you are responsible for. Just like everyone of your employees. And your employees need to know what your role is. You need to do your job and let them do theirs.

YOUR JOB DESCRIPTION

In making up your job description, you need to know what you do best for the business. Don't assign yourself a duty you can't do or do poorly. In the Al's Seafood example, Chad was trying to take care of all the bookkeeping because that was what his dad used to do. Robert finally put Chad's sister on that instead and Chad was put to work managing the employees. These new role assignments were a much better fit for Chad and Cara. They were happier, less stressed and much more successful in what they were doing.

Remember: You need to be working on the business, not in it. Your job description should reflect this. Depending on the size, structure, and maturity of your business, you may have to work in the business. If you do, you will be putting those duties in your job description—just make sure they do not conflict with what your employees should be doing.

Your assignment this week:

- Make up your own job description (if you don't have one already)
- Review your job description (if you already have one)
- Do this on an annual basis or whenever you make changes in your business structure that would affect your role

Imagine your business as a play with you and your employees as the actors. The better everyone knows their roles and plays them well, the more the audience (your clientele) will appreciate the play. They will show their appreciation by coming back to see you and your team often. Everyone loves a good play!

See you next week when we play with your Margins.

CHAPTER 14

WEEK 13—MARGINS: SET THEM ACCORDINGLY TO ACHIEVE YOUR PROFIT GOALS

"I don't want to do business with those who don't make a profit, because they can't give the best service."

—LEE BRISTOL

What is one commodity that almost every person who shops for groceries knows the price of? Milk! Eggs and bread are next on that list. According to a report from Cleveland.com, the average gross profit on a half-gallon of milk varies from .04 to .22 cents per gallon. [18]If this is one commodity that everyone buys, why price it so low? Because it gets customers into the store when it is priced competitively. Once they get there, they will end up buying many other items that have higher profit margins that offset the low ones on milk and other key staples.

"Years ago, a University of Chicago study showed that the average consumer only knew the prices of about 13 supermarket items out of 30,000 being offered. Milk was one of those items," said Eugene Fram, professor emeritus of marketing at the Rochester Institute of Technology's E. Philip Saunders College of Business.

There are two messages here on pricing. First is that commodity items such as milk tend to be purchased on price only. Second is that survey after survey have shown that quality and convenience are #1 and #2, with price usually around #4 or #5 on the list when it comes to people's buying habits and decisions.[19] How would this apply to your business? You need to have variable margins for different products, but you need to add value in the process. However, the focus of

---

18   Roger Mezger, Milk is No Cash Cow for Grocery Stores (Cleveland News) https://bit.ly/2OVQKOt Aug 24, 2008

19   Classification of Buying Motives: Product Buying and Patronage Buying https://bit.ly/2HN7iG3

this chapter is that many businesses use variable margins to attain their profit goals.

THE LITTLE GUITAR PICK

A good friend of mine, ActionCoach Bruce Wilson, told me the story of a Guitar store owner he worked with who complained that he wasn't making enough money and was barely able to keep the doors open. During the process of reviewing his business, he asked the owner what were the most popular items that he sold and at what profit margins. The most popular item the store sold was guitar picks—he sold hundreds of them every month. The cost was $0.25, and he sold them for $0.50. Bruce proposed that the owner sell them for $0.95. The result was no decline in sales and the store made a couple hundred more dollars each month! This was just the start of the transformation of the business as they implemented price increases on other items.

Many businesses, like the guitar store, use the simple formula of charging double the cost of almost every item sold to the customer. Simple, but this does not help them make the money they need to make a decent living (remember the income stats in my introduction?).

DON'T JUST USE THE LIST PRICE

Many businesses do just like I used to do: use the list price for the many products resold. My accountant counseled me on what the margins should be, based on industry averages and on several of the categories of the products I sold. So, I adjusted the margins accordingly to match the averages. Then in a business workshop I attended, I learned about a pricing strategy called Matrix pricing, which consists of a higher markup for the lowest cost items to a lower margin on the highest cost items. The margins are set up on a graduated basis for certain cost quadrants. This helped my bottom line immensely and added consistency and simplification of the markup process.

The big idea of a margins matrix is that most people worry about the cost of the higher dollar or most popular items over the smaller, lower cost, or impulse items. If you balk at charging more for many items, consider this: many businesses have been using this strategy very successfully for many years. If you want to make more money, you need to adopt new ways to transform your business practices.

Your assignment this week:

- Figure out what the average markups for your industry are. Check out this article on several retail markups: https://bit.ly/32hdBIj

- Determine which markup strategy works for you a: Matrix or a variable.
- What might be your loss leader product (milk) in your business?
- What might be your high volume, high margin product (guitar picks)?
- Adjust your prices accordingly
- How can you systematize this in a way that everyone in your business can follow it? (Matrix is best for this.)
- What other high margin products can you sell in your business as a complement to your current mix?
- Review this on an annual basis. The Matrix concept usually won't change, but you may need to look at product mix and variables based on demand, sales volumes, and loss leaders.

Now that you are making more money, you should be anxious to see what's in store for next week.

CHAPTER 15

WEEKT 14—THE 5 WHYS: TOOLS FOR PROBLEM SOLVING

———

"Problem solving is hunting. It is savage pleasure and we are born to it."

—THOMAS HARRIS

Imagine you are 4 years old again. How much do you know about the world? Not much. When you don't understand something that you see or are told to do or not to do, you ask a simple question: Why? And you ask the same question over and over until you are satisfied with the answer (or until the adult has had enough of your questions!). Simple, but asking why is a great method to understand your problem, its root cause, and come up with some solution(s).

As a business owner, you have many small decisions to make every day, but sometimes you have bigger decisions to make or issues to address that will take some time to resolve. You need some tools to help you when it comes to making key decisions. This week's assignment is learning the decision-making tools that will help you with the many components of running a business and the inevitable problems that will arise.

THE 5 WHYS TOOL

The 5 Whys was formally developed in the 1930s by Sakichi Toyoda, a Japanese inventor and industrialist; the technique then became an integral part of the Lean philosophy.[20] This process is still used today by Toyota and many other companies around the world. Many businesses use this, or similarly developed processes, in goal setting and general decision making.

The process is quite simple. You can use it for your business or personal problem solving. Engaging your team is recommended in addressing anything that relates to them. They

---

20   Wikipedia, Five Whys https://bit.ly/2osUMTU

can help answer the "5 *Why questions*" by adding their perspectives on the issue(s). Asking 5 Why questions will usually reveal the root problem so you can come up with a solution. You may find your answers in less than five or you may need to keep asking a few more. But take caution in asking too many Why questions as one can get off track. Remember you are trying to find the root cause of your well-defined problem.

Here is a sample exercise:

- The problem is: The customer gave us a 1-star review.
    - Why?—The project was completed way past the promised date.
    - Why?—It took us longer than we thought.
    - Why?—We ran out of supplies.
    - Why?—The supplies we were going to use had already been allocated to another project.
    - Why?—We didn't have enough in stock to meet the demand and it took longer than expected to get more supplies.
- Some solutions could be to increase stock of supplies, find another vendor wtho can give real-time deliveries, or set realistic expectations with customers. What others could you come up with?

You can see the simplicity of using this method. This can be on your own, in a simple meeting with your team or in a more formal meeting led by a 3rd party like your business coach, mentor or other advisor. After the root cause is clearly defined you will brainstorm on solutions. Depending on the type of determined solution you should consider adding it to your policy and procedures manual.

"Being flexible means to explore alternative ways to solve problems. Never think there is a short list of solutions you can pick from."—Pearl Zhu

There are many other tools for problem solving and decision making. You don't have to settle for just one tool as the decisions you have to make vary and may require different methods to resolve them.

- The 5 Ws: Who, What, Where, When, and Why questions. You can add 'How?' to this list, as well. They constitute a formula for getting the complete story on a subject or situation. They could be used for staffing, project management, and more
- Simple T chart Method: Take a piece of paper, draw a horizontal line across the top of the page about 0.5 inches below the top, then a line down the middle of the page. On the top line, write *"Plus"* on one side of the vertical line and *"Minus"* on the other side. You make a list of all the pluses and minuses of the issue you must decide on. It could be about a purchase, an employee, a location to

move to, or more. This is a simple way to bring clarity to a 'yes' or 'no' decision.

- Decision Matrix: Like the T chart, but this is used when you have several options for your decision. Use this for something like buying a piece of equipment from several different manufacturers, or a possible move of your business to one of several locations. The matrix could be easily made using a spreadsheet where you have the options listed on the rows and the various ratings or options available on the columns. Here is a link to a great site to help you with this process: https://bit.ly/1KRvmjo
- S.W.O.T. Analysis: Strengths, weaknesses, opportunities, and threats. This is a great tool for business planning and review. This is covered in more detail in Week 50.

There are many great sites online that can give you more details on these tools and more. Here is one site that lists some of the above as well as a few other options for decision making: https://bit.ly/31pQzyS

Your assignment this week:

- If you have a pending issue or decision you have been putting off for lack of a tool, choose one and address it this week.
- Review the available tools and choose the one(s) that work best for your business.

- Refer to these as the need arises.

Decision making and problem solving is part of your job description as the owner. These tools should make your job a lot easier.

I'll close with an appropriate quote: *"When a problem comes along, study it until you are completely knowledgeable. Then find that weak spot, break the problem apart, and the rest will be easy."*—Norman Vincent Peale

See you next week when we talk about the World Wide Web and your place in it.

CHAPTER 16

WEEK 15—YOUR WEBSITE: THE FLAGSHIP OF YOUR MARKETING

"A website is a window through which your business says hello to the world."

—AMIT KALANTRIS

When people are looking for your business online, can they find it quickly and easily, even if they don't type in your exact business name?

I do a workshop called *"11.5 Ways to Massively Grow Your Customer Base in 30-60 Days."* It's all about marketing your business on many fronts to bring in new clientele. One of the methods I share, of course, is using the internet and having a website. You might respond with a *"Duh, who wouldn't?!"* I once did this workshop for a local Chamber of Commerce where over fifty business owners were in attendance. When I came to the part of the presentation about web presence, I paused a moment and asked, *"How many of you have a website?"* Only half of the attendees raised their hands! And this was in Silicon Valley of all places! *"Why don't some of you have a website?"* I asked. Some stated they felt they were too small to have a website while others used platforms like Yelp or Facebook. While Facebook and Yelp do help you get discovered, you will be crowded out by others who have a website that is current and has activity. A current website that is up to date, has activity and is well optimized are what all the search engines are looking for.

SOME CRITERIA FOR A WELL PERFORMING WEBSITE

Ever been to a site the takes too long to load or is confusing or cluttered? There are several items that are important to have a good website. The parameters for each of these change as does their importance for search. Below is a list with a simple explanation of each.

- Performance
    - Optimizing your website's performance is crucial to increasing traffic, improving conversion rates, generating more leads, and increasing revenue. Ever been to a site that takes forever (5 seconds!) to load? Your prospects won't wait that long either!
- Mobile friendly
    - Traffic from mobile devices is growing fast. As of the writing of this book, mobile search accounts for almost 60 percent of all searches. Optimize your website for mobile or you'll miss out on valuable traffic, leads, and revenue. Include the verbiage of a mobile search query on your site. An app is not required for people to find you!
- SEO—Search Engine Optimization
    - Make sure your website is easy for users to discover—and easy for search engines to understand—with better page titles, headings, and meta descriptions.
- SEM—Search Engine Marketing
    - This is really a part of SEO, but it is not always necessary. It is hypervisibility. This would include paid search and banner ads.
- Security
    - SSL certificates protect websites from attacks and give visitors confidence that your site is authentic

and trustworthy. I have seen many sites that were hacked and directed people to other sites. Look for the little lock next to the URL

- Platform
    - Use the latest platform like WordPress. If your site was built many years ago, the above parameters may not work well, if at all.

HIRE A PROFESSIONAL

Unless one of your relatives is a professional and is willing to keep your site up to date, go out and pay someone to build one for you. Make sure they can help with the criteria listed above. Don't make a barter deal—pay someone—it is much easier to fire them if they don't perform. (I've seen this happen all too often.) The best professionals charge at least $2,500 to build a good website and $100 a month to maintain it. A good site must be maintained, or it will slowly drift off the first pages of the search engines—a good reason to hire that professional. Other changes happen like the ADA compliance standards (effective in 2010) now suggested for all websites. I know a fair amount about this topic, but I don't have the expertise nor the time to do my own site. That is why I hired someone to build and maintain my site.

You may have to do some research, ask for some referrals, and look at some of the pages of your competitors to see what you are up against. Do they have good web hosting servers that work reliably 24/7? And just what is the goal of your website? Make sure you have this in mind while working with your web designer. If you are part of a business or industry association, you may be able to get some help there or investigate a designer that specializes in your industry. Or maybe one of your vendors may have a solution for you that works with your Customer Relationship Manager (CRM) or Point Of Sale (POS) software programs.

A few other considerations

- Your web presence is a big part of your marketing and it must be congruent with your other marketing pieces. You must keep the same theme and target market if it is to be effective.
- Coupons, promotions, and specials—change them at least quarterly and make the offers slightly different than the promotions you may be running in other places.
- Have a Careers section—you should always be looking for new employees. See
- Week 29 on Hiring.
- Tracking—you need to be able to get reports on how well the site is doing for you ('click-throughs', calls, sales generated, etc.) and checking them regularly.
- Your business name, location, and contact information should be one of the first things seen on the page. Best to

have it on the top and bottom of each page. Sometimes that is all the visitor is looking for.

- Have a unique phone number for tracking the calls (some website/marketing services will do this for you).
- Make sure any photos of your business and/or team match what your prospect will see when they come to meet you.

Your assignment for this week:

- Get a website if you don't have one! Best to hire this out. (see suggestions above.)
- Meet with your website designer/host to discuss what's new and how to make your site better.
- Schedule other items you might want to update from time to time, such as new employees, refresh coupons, etc.

As I mentioned earlier, the web changes quickly and your site should follow those changes.

See you next week—it's something to talk about!

CHAPTER 17

WEEK 16—TALK GUIDELINES

——

"Only the prepared speaker deserves to be confident."

—DALE CARNEGIE

A local competing service business was closing. Carlos wanted those customers, so he made a deal to purchase the phone number of that business. But customers got confused when calling in and hearing a greeting from his existing business. He decided it was best for anyone answering the phones to use a generic greeting for all calls. (He should have had the number set up on a separate phone line to be able to properly ID the callers.) This increased the conversion rate as the prospective customer did not hang up immediately.

The staff now had the time to explain the new ownership of the customer base.

When I started working with him, I noticed his manager answered calls like this: *"Hello, this is Greg!"* Now if you were to call in for the first time or if you were an existing customer that did not know Greg, what would you think? Questions like, *"What company is this?"* or, *"Who is Greg?"* might come to mind. I can understand Carlos' original thinking about the basic greeting, but he had made the purchase of the customer base several years earlier! It was time to come up with a much better greeting.

WHAT ARE THEY SAYING?

How do your calls get answered? Is it the same every time? Or do you and everyone else that answers the phones do so however they feel like? Or how about when a customer enters your place of business? Every interaction with a client or prospect (and vendors) should have a talk track. Some might call this scripting, after all, we are trying to convey a standard message and are on *"stage"* every time we interact with clients.

Guidelines should be made up for every conversation with the customer, especially how everyone answers the phone. Consistency is key and builds confidence in your team members. Also, what is the last thing the customer hears as they leave the business at the end of every transaction? This is key to how they will think of the business after they leave. The goal is to make sure it is not only pleasant, but memorable. Some conversation tips:

- Smile! Any and all conversations—yes, even those on the phone—should be done with a smile on the face of you and your employees. It really does make for a more pleasant-sounding conversation.
- Listen! This is the most critical of all mantras in talking with customers. In building your talk track, make a space for pauses and to repeat back what the customer is saying at the appropriate times. It helps to verify what the customer is saying and lets them know they are being listened to.
- Use their name! Whenever appropriate use their name: the sweetest thing they love to hear. Use it when they first introduce themselves: *"Nice to meet you, Jeffrey!"*
- Build rapport. When the customers mention anything that is not business-related, ask about it or weave the topic into the conversation, but do so as a natural part of your conversation.

CALL TRACKING

Since many of the interactions with your clients take place over the phone, recording calls is a must. This will help you check in on how your employees are handling calls without you having to stand by them all the time. The other advantage is to be able to review the calls with your employees. Ever record yourself in a customer interaction and listen to it later? If you are like me, you will be surprised by some of the habits you have unknowingly acquired. The same goes for your employees. If you don't have a service that does this for you already, maybe it's time to do so this week. Some marketing companies include this in their services.

SAMPLE PHONE GREETINGS

"Good morning! AAA Sewing Machine and Vacuum, this is Jeff, how may I help you today?"

"Hello! This is Susan of Valley Carpet and Floor Cleaning Services. How may I help you get your carpets cleaner?"

"Good Afternoon! You have reached the law offices of Fredrickson and Jones. This is Asha. How may I help you?"

A sample greeting when someone enters the store:

"Good afternoon! Welcome to Celia's Antiques. My name is Celia. Have you been here before? Can I give you a tour of our store?"

A sample outgoing call:

"Hello! This is Aaron of Stelling Insurance Agency. I would like to speak with Ms. Farnsworth about her policies. Is she available?"

A sample talk track at the close of the sale/purchase (also known as *"the sale, after the sale"*):

"Here are the clothes we cleaned for you. Four shirts, one skirt and three dress slacks. We made sure any and all stains were treated and removed. Thanks for trusting us to keep your clothes looking great!"

"Thank you for your purchase today. All our products come with a money back guarantee. If you have any problems, don't hesitate to call or bring the product back so we can address your concerns. We look forward to seeing you again soon."

"Thank you so much for dining with us today/tonight. We hope you enjoyed your meal as much as we enjoyed serving you."

YOUR SALES PROCESS

How does your team sell? What do they say when attempting to sell your product or service? How do they handle objections, price shoppers, technical requests, and more? No matter what process you use, you should have guidelines on what to say, how to say it and when to say it.

If you need additional help with your sales process, I suggest you investigate several great sales books (listed in the Appendix and on www.1week1thing). You should be able to find a book that fits your business. You can attend classes—look to your business association(s)—or hire a sales coach or trainer. The best advice I can offer is once you find a sales process that works for you and your team, stick with it and practice it with your team members often until it becomes second nature.

Two more tips in building these talk tracks:

- Be aware of all those conversations you have as you make transactions with other businesses. It is OK to adapt the good ones into your own business.
- Use layman's terms when talking to customers. Coach your people not to use industry acronyms. CIGNA insurance employees once used the term EOB (short for *"Explanation of Benefits"*) when referring to an insurance report form sent to customers after an office visit. It confused the customers a lot since they knew it as the *"This Is Not A Bill"* form—the very words at the top of the form and not an EOB.

Your assignment this week is:

- First—make a list of all the customer interactions that should have talking guidelines. The phone calls in and out, the order taking, the presentation of the invoice, the discussion on closing a sale, the prospecting call, and more.
- Second—prioritize the list by most important talk tracks, such as answering the phone.
- Starting with the top three, make talk tracks for these calls/scenarios.

Schedule some time to complete more of the list over the next few months. Do them *"on the fly."* Seek out help from your employees.

You should put all these into your employee handbook so everyone will have these the day they get hired. Your team will look more professional and your customer loyalty will soar.

Next week is all about making things easy.

CHAPTER 18

WEEK 17—MAKE IT EASY TO BUY FROM YOU

———

"Make your product easier to buy than your competition, or you will find your customers buying from them, not you."

—MARK CUBAN

I was waiting to meet a client at his business to assist with his software program. I wanted to be there when he opened so I could get a jump on helping him with an update and do some training. It was 8 a.m. and the shop was still closed, even though his website indicated that he opened at that time. While I waited for him, I noticed a woman drive onto his lot, get out of her car and go to the front door, then after realizing the shop was still not open, get back into her car and drive off.

The owner showed up about 8:25 a.m. to open the shop and start about his business. Ten minutes later the woman who had stopped by earlier showed up. She greeted him, asked about getting a specific service done that his website offered, then made a statement about the hours on the website and him not being open at that hour. His response was that he made a change in opening times and that was noted on the door to the business. No real apology, just a plain statement. She did not say anything else, except to get what she came for and then left. I doubt she ever returned for any other services. Would you?

I share this story because at the time of this incident, the first thing that came to mind was the quote at the start of this chapter. I often wonder why many business owners make themselves so difficult to buy from. Why do we not step back and look for all those little things that complicate the process of doing business? Many times, when a customer or prospect asks, *"Why?"* they are telling us it is difficult for them to buy. Confusion creates inaction on the part of the customer, so they don't buy at all. The questions we should ask ourselves: *"Why are they asking this question?"* and *"Why are they making such a statement?"* Before the customer asks these questions, we need to ask ourselves: *"How can I make things easier for my customers to buy from me?"*

Harry Beckwith wrote in his best-selling book *Selling The Invisible*, many aren't looking for the best, but the easiest or most convenient to buy from.[21]

WHAT'S KEEPING THEM AWAY FROM YOU?

This is the week to take stock of all the things that might be making it difficult for clientele to buy from you. It usually is not big things, but most likely the very small things like the example of the shop with mismatched hours of operation.

Here are a few things to consider:

- The address of your business. How many times have you been looking for a business while driving down a street where there are few readable addresses? When I first purchased my service station, I put the address in 12-inch-sized numbers over the front door as there were no numbers anywhere on the building before!
- Your website and Social Media pages. Does your website load quickly and is it mobile friendly? Is your contact information prominently displayed on the first page? (See Week 15.)
- Your emails, or any other online contact: Are your email and/or website link(s) easy to find? Are they *"clickable"*?

---

26 Harry Beckwith, Selling the Invisible (New York: Warner Books, 1997) 93-93

I recently received an email from a company without a web address or link. I was interested in buying something but moved on. Your prospects may be doing the same.

- Your operating hours. Are they well displayed on the premises and on ALL your web and social media sites? Are the hours the same on all sites and do they match those on your premises?
- Your people. How are they greeting and handling new and existing customers? Make sure they are not using industry terms and acronyms but talking in layman's terms. More of this is covered in the Week 16.
- Pricing of products and/or services. Ever been to a store where the prices are missing from the product? How about getting a quote for some service that lacks clarity and leads to many more questions?
- Access to your premises. If parking is an issue (no parking on the street, special parking garage, etc.) how can you address this to make it more convenient for the prospective customer to get to you? Is a map displayed on all your online pages?

Your assignment this week:

- Review the above list and take note of the things that may make it difficult for your prospects and customers to do business with you.

- Get some help with this by asking some of your best customers or mentors for their thoughts.
- Seek out feedback from your employees.
- Once you have the list, implement the changes.

Repeat this activity annually or whenever you get a customer asking, *"Why?"* about something you do when that should be obvious.

See you next week where we really clean things up!

CHAPTER 19

WEEK 18—CLEAN THE BUSINESS

———

"How you do anything is indicative of how you do everything."

—JEFFREY NOTT

When you are traveling in the car with small children, stops at many of the roadside establishments are a given. There were times we'd make a restroom stop where my wife and daughters came right back out of the restaurant and informed me that we needed to find another stop as the restrooms were uninhabitable! We decided not to stay for a meal. If they can't keep the restrooms clean, can they be trusted to properly clean the kitchen and serve safe food? We made a note never to stop there again. In our travels, we discovered certain places, predominantly a few chains, that were the most reliable for good food and clean restrooms.

What about your business? When was the last time you stopped and gave your place of business a good look over from a customer's point of view? Even if you are only a one-person business, what is the first thing people see when they enter your office? Or your vehicle? What you may not 'see' speaks volumes to your clientele about how you do things.

How about this scenario: You come to pick up your vehicle at the local garage. Your spouse refuses to sit on the chairs in the waiting room because they are not very clean and is afraid of soiling her clothes. What thoughts may go through your minds? *"Hmm, if the chairs are dirty, how will they keep my vehicle from getting grease marks? What will be the quality of the repairs?"* This little thing, dirty chairs, reflects badly on the business. Image is everything, no matter how much society says we should not be judged by appearances. Human nature cannot be denied. In a world of ever-increasing competition, you need to keep your appearance more acceptable than ever.

The week's task is about cleaning up your business and setting up a cleaning schedule. This may include hiring a cleaning company to help you keep up with the schedule. It may mean doing some work that is not necessarily your responsibility.

For example: There is an Applebee's restaurant near me that keeps their landscape and parking lot very well maintained. They have the gardeners take care of the area of the local freeway offramp alongside their building, as well. They understand the value of doing so.

Whether you have a retail, high tech office or home-based business, I have an inspection sheet for you at www.1week-1thing.com to use as every business needs some cleaning. I suggest you ask your spouse or neighbor or good customer to help you go through the list and give you an honest opinion. There is this thing called *"olfactory fatigue"* when one no longer notices the smells in their environment. As business owners we tend to get the same way, sort of a visual blindness to our environment, so we need the outside opinion of others. We should make sure our prospects and customers see our business in a positive manner.

One more thing to consider: your employees. If your place is not so attractive to your prospects and customers, how would that affect your employees? The better the workplace is, the higher the productivity, morale, and longevity of your team! This could also lead to a reduction of workplace injuries and insurance costs.

Other than clean furniture and restrooms, what other areas should you address? Here are a few areas to consider:

- Condition of the building—paint condition, cleanliness of walls, windows, doors, carpets, etc.
- Condition of the parking area—potholes, paving, parking stripes, places to park, etc.
- Landscape—trimmed, maintained, no trees/vegetation blocking the visibility, etc.
- Office/waiting area/reception—clean, bright, free of clutter, new magazines (please no industry news—offer magazines your clients want to read)
- Workspaces—just like the reception area, well lit, organized, inventory easy to access, etc.
- Windows—if you have a display window, keep it clean and have fresh displays, don't block out the view into the store completely. Seasonal window painting needs to be just that, seasonal—remove anything out of date. Too many posters and displays just become visual noise so keep them to a minimum. Remove any out-of-date or tired banners and signs.
- Employee-only area/break room—keep required posters up to date and get rid of anything not current; keep the area clean and pleasant.
- Banners, flags, displays—these get old and unseen after forty-five to ninety days, remove or rearrange to keep interest and catch the eyes of the passerby.
- Lighting—inside and out—should all be working and attractive.
- More suggestions can be found at my website.

Your goals for this week:

- Do a facilities inspection.
- Set up what needs to be addressed immediately then schedule the rest.
- Set up a cleaning/maintenance schedule: what needs to be done daily, weekly, monthly, yearly, and/or every so many years.
- Hire a cleaning crew or maintenance company to help, if you don't already have this.

The bottom line of this exercise (clean up) can really improve your bottom line.

See you next week when we start to create some great experiences.

CHAPTER 20

WEEK 19—CREATE A GREAT CUSTOMER EXPERIENCE

"Remember that at the end of the day, it's not what you say or what you do, but how you make people feel that matters the most."

—TONY HSIEH, CO-FOUNDER OF ZAPPOS

When the Saturn Car company first started, they did a lot to make raving fans of their customers. A good friend of mine that worked at a local dealership shared his experiences while working there. One of the most impressive stories of exceptional customer experience was the procedure of giving the keys to a new vehicle owner. After the paperwork was completed and the vehicle was detailed and prepped for delivery, all the dealership staff were called into the showroom where the vehicle was waiting. As the salesman handed the keys to the new owners, all the staff cheered, gave whistles, and clapped their hands. He told me it was quite a spectacle to be a part of and remembers it very fondly. Imagine the feeling and memory that was created for the new car owner. Saturn had a record of very loyal customers.

Another fun thing they did was have free coffee and donuts in their lobbies available for any customer, whether they were there for service or not. I remember the story of a college student visiting every Saturn dealership on his way back home from college. They really did create a unique culture. Yes, General Motors eventually closed Saturn for other economic reasons, but their legacy lives on in other dealerships and in the fond memories of many Saturn owners.

HOW DO YOU STAND OUT?

What do you do to make any transaction more than just that? What do you do to stand out from all the others in your industry when many consumers see most products and services as basically the same? You may rebuke this statement with a response like, *"I do a better job than anyone else!"* That may be true, but can your clientele really tell a difference?

Many businesses these days lament the internet for creating a consumer culture of price as the driving force in buying anything. Yet, survey after survey of what drives consumer choice in buying something shows that price usually falls between No. 4 and No. 7 on that list. Why then, is the first thing a prospect asks, *"How much?"* It's because they have little knowledge of the differences in the products or services available. You must educate them, but more importantly, you must generate a better experience in the very first interaction with them. (See Week 16 – Talk Guidelines.)

The old saying *"Under promise and over deliver"* is the key here. I once toured the Zappos headquarters in Las Vegas and encourage every business owner to make the time to do so, if visiting the area. During the tour, they share a lot about their culture, but creating a great customer experience is the main theme. One way they give something unexpected is when someone places an order with a three- to five-day delivery time, they make sure the shipment arrives in two days! *"Deliver WOW through customer service"* is No. 1 on Zappos' list of company values.[22]

No matter what you deliver, you can do something to stand out and create a raving fan of your client. And just what is a raving fan? They are those that are so happy doing business

---

27   Hsieh, *Delivering Happiness*, 154

with you that they tell many others about you without you asking them to do so.

Here are just a few things you can do to make a real difference:

- Wall of new customer photos—in your office and/or online.
- Extended warranties or warranty something just out of warranty.
- Easy return or exchange of items purchased.
- Follow-up calls after a purchase.
- Food/goodie basket as a thank you gift.
- Special advice/news they could use (educate them).
- Thank them for a great review (always).
- Send out holiday, seasonal, birthday, and/or 'special' day cards.
- An unexpected discount for future purchases.
- Thank You card—not the automated one (which everyone should have)—the handwritten kind!
- Some industry specific ideas:
  - Restaurant—something extra at no cost—one very popular Italian restaurant near me gives a free limoncello for dessert.
  - Dealership/auto service—wash the car after servicing, free ride-share/taxi ride to or from the shop.

- Home repairs—leave the place much cleaner than when you arrived, maybe have a house-keeper come in after the construction.
- Major kitchen appliance repairs—dining gift card while the repairs are being made.
- Salon—glass of champagne (check with local laws on this), fine chocolates, foot massages, etc.
- Insurance—gift card for something related to the policy—car wash for car insurance, hardware store gift card for home insurance.

- More ideas can be found on my website www.1week1thing.com. And feel free to share what works for you at jeff@1week1thing.com
- Here is a link to a great article on twenty-five ways to thank your customers to create a better experience for them: https://bit.ly/2H6NnQn
- Here is a link to some stories of excellent customer service: https://bit.ly/2kHACy6

What I have not covered in this chapter is you and your staff—everyone is the key to making sure your customer has a great experience. This is covered in Week 21, but I will say this here: treat your employees like you want them to treat your clientele.

Your assignment this week:

- Come up with some ways to enhance your customer experience to really stand out of the crowd.
- Schedule time to train and implement the strategy you have chosen to your team.
- Review this at least once a year.

This should be a fun exercise and your success will be written on the faces of your customers.

See you next week where we get social.

CHAPTER 21

WEEK 20—SOCIAL MEDIA: YOU MUST EMBRACE IT

———

"I was going to post something on Facebook until I asked myself why."

—DAVID E LOVE, JOURNALIST

When I started my coaching business years ago, I had a professional website built with all the SEO, metatags, links, and key words to help boost my search results. But I knew I had to do more. As I mentioned in Week 15, Google and other search engines love activity. I was already on Facebook personally but built a separate business page. I joined Instagram, Twitter,

Pinterest, Snapchat, Google+ (now defunct), and have been on LinkedIn for many years. I posted some YouTube videos. Why do all this? To increase my web presence. It worked! If you did a search for *"Business Coach San Jose"* (or something similar) I was on the first page under several different headings. I did all this without spending money for key words or banner ads. What it took was being diligent about posting on various social media sites on a regular basis.

I could spend a lot of time delving deep into this subject (sort of like, *"I'm just going to check in on Facebook for a few minutes."*) but I will endeavor to keep it as simple as possible.

Like it or loathe it, social media has an impact on your business, and you need to take advantage of its power.

The need to engage is at an all-time high. That's because a recent Sprout Social study showed that 48% of consumers prefer buying from brands that are attentive and responsive to their customers via social media. Willingness to digitally engage helps instill trust which makes consumers more likely to buy. [23]People buy from those they know, like and trust.

28 Nathan MendenHall, A Data-driven Look at What Consumers Want From Brands on Social Media (Blog: Social Media Today, 2019) https://bit.ly/2NQYU7B

WHERE TO BEGIN?

To help you with this, you should seek out an expert. Whoever does your website would be my first suggestion to talk with. They may be able to help you or recommend someone for you. Or you could go it alone, maybe to start, if your budget is tight (See Week 4—Know your Numbers).

Before you just jump in and post everywhere, you need to know which sites are best for you to be active on. Which sites are your customers on? You should be on more than one platform. I suggest you get a page on the top five and any site that is related to your industry. You don't have to post on all of them all the time, just the few most related to your endeavors—and drop any that don't get you any feedback.

GO WHERE THE FISH ARE.

Those who like to fish know where to find them and what bait and tackle works best. The same goes with social media. Which sites do your clients (and prospects) spend time on? You will be able to tell when you get feedback from your target audience. That is the best way to narrow down your choices. Still not sure? There is a lot of information on the internet, but I came across this site, which has some very good information and info-graphics to help the reader make some educated choices: https://bit.ly/33G5vcD

Some examples of which sites are best for what:

- LinkedIn—best for business-to-business interactions. If you are a trainer, CEO, or other leader, this is all business. Political posts are not welcome here. You will find most posts are business articles or inspirational ones that help the reader (and promote the poster).
- Facebook—best for social interactions of all kinds. Advertising on this site is getting bigger by the day. Social events, live podcasts, and other similar content are welcome here. Not a great place if you are looking to reach those under 20.
- Twitter—is a blend of real time social media, blogging, and texting. You will find posts of all topics.
- Pinterest—has the largest audience of women of all social media platforms. Picture-centric posts. A visual social network. It has been called a *"digital scrapbook."*
- Instagram—is a social networking app made for sharing photos and videos from a smartphone. This one cannot be automated like the others, but it is gaining popularity every day. Depending on your business, you may have to be very creative to use it. It is now the No. 2 social network.
- YouTube—best for creating videos about your business and how you do it. Really helps to get you found as it is now the No. 2 search engine.

PLAN YOUR POSTINGS

Managing social media takes more than fifteen minutes a day. This is true whether you work for an agency or brand, or you own your own business. There are tools to help you post on many sites at the same time. This link has a good rundown of the top tools: https://bit.ly/2nuLWR2 Or you could hire another company to do so for you. Many marketing companies offer packages to manage all or most of your internet activity.

One of the challenges with social media is that is it difficult to track the effectiveness of your postings to the bottom-line of your business. Avoid the *"Vanity Metric"*—getting a lot of likes. Many of those likes may not be your customers. To be able to track a true ROI on social media, you need to buy ads or boosts for your posts. Paid ads will give you tracking reports. Try your best to put a unique offering, such as *"asks"* for likes and shares, and use *"mentions"* of your posts for the prospect to get business discounts or specials.

And what to post? Look at what your competitors post. Best to keep regular posts social—that's why it's called social media.

Here is a list of *"5 Ways to Build Your Brand on Social Media"* from Germany Kent[24] for you to contemplate:

1. Post content that adds value.

2. Spread positivity.

3. Create a steady stream of info.

4. Make an impact.

5. Be yourself.

Your assignment this week:

- Narrow down the social media platforms to work with and/or seek out a social media specialist to help you.
- Schedule time to post to sites on a regular basis. Decide if you want to automate this by using a tool listed at https://bit.ly/2nuLWR2.

There are industry-specific companies that can do a lot of the *"heavy lifting"* for you. Check with your association or your POS/CRM software provider for help.

---

249 Germany Kent, 5 Ways to Build Your Brand on Social Media (Goodreads, 2019) https://bit.ly/31qgUvx

You should revisit these choices and plans on an annual basis as, like everything else these days, change happens quickly in the Internet world.

I'll close this chapter with an appropriate quote:

"Be a person that others will look for your posts daily because they know you will encourage them. Be the positive one and help others to have a great day and you will find that not only do they like you, but you will like you too."

—JOHN PATRICK HICKEY, OOPS! DID I REALLY POST THAT

Up next week: more on helping your team achieve more.

CHAPTER 22

WEEK 21—TEAM GOALS: HELPING YOUR TEAM HELPS YOUR BUSINESS

———

"You will get all you want in life if you help enough other people get what they want."

—ZIG ZIGLAR

When Adrian was first hired at the UPS store, he was your typical employee: He didn't really understand business or customer service. His employer, Ravinder, put it this way: *"He was a bit rough around the edges when he started."* Adrian just needed a job to make some money while going to school at the local Art school. What he really wanted to do was learn a lot more about videography, not business.

At the first company party that Adrian attended, Ravinder asked him, *"What's the most important thing to do for our customers?"* Adrian's response was *"Get all the money you can from every customer!"* This is hardly the focus of the type of customer service that Ravinder wanted from his staff. Ravinder knew he had some work to do with Adrian to embrace the company culture of customer service.

FOCUS ON OTHERS' GOALS

Ravinder Lal is the owner of four successful UPS stores in the Silicon Valley area. In the present economy of the lowest unemployment on record, he is fully staffed and has very loyal employees. He shared with me this focus on building up his team members. His attitude is that it's not what they can do for him, but about how he can help them on their journey. With an attitude like that, what employee would be anxious to leave him?

Ravinder sensed that Adrian's genuine interest in videography and encouraged him to pursue it. He got Adrian some coaching from a business coach and others to help him do more. Ravinder truly feels that he is there to inspire his people to do more and be more.

The end result of Ravinder's focus on helping Adrian? He not only became a much better employee but stayed with him for five years and when he got married made sure to invite Ravinder to attend. They met up a year or two later for dinner. When Ravinder went to pay the bill, Adrian took it away from him and said, *"You no longer have to get my tab. I am making over $300,000 a year and can afford to pay for your meal. Thank you!"*

GOAL SETTING MEETING

This week's assignment is setting up a meeting to help your team to set and achieve their own goals. How do you do this? There are several ways. The more tedious task is to ask each of them to share them with you one on one. The other, more efficient way is to dedicate a team meeting just for goal setting.

- Before the meeting you should prep the employees about what the purpose of the meeting is—for all, including you, the goal is to share their goals and plan for them—and the preparation they should make beforehand.
- Start with some simple talk about dreams, goals, plans and more. You may want to bring in a guest speaker (could be your coach, a Toastmaster, or other business leader) to facilitate for you. (I did this for several youth groups as a young man—would have been happy if

someone outside my groups asked me to facilitate such a meeting).

- Bring in a financial planner sometime for a special meeting.
- Ask for a volunteer to share first, but if no one wants to start, you lead by sharing your goal for starting the business. You can start out small to get the team to open up. It may be difficult for many to open up but keep working at it.
- TAKE NOTES so you can refer to these later in the meeting and in future meetings. You may want to assign this to an employee if you are the facilitator.
- Tie the funding of their personal goals to the attainment of their employment goals—this is a team effort. Many of the individuals' company goals should have been given to them the day they were hired. These numbers are covered in several other chapters.
- The goal of this exercise is to show your team that working for you is not all about your business and/or personal goals. You want to show your interest in helping them achieve their own goals and that the business is just one way to help them get to where they want to go.

There is much on the internet on how to hold a meeting like this, but these are the basics. Here's a link to 5 Goal Setting Activities: https://bit.ly/2l26FOM You will find more information and forms at my website www.1week1thing.com

One more tip: whenever you hire a new employee, part of the process of on-boarding should be to find out what their goals are, personal and professional, and how together, both of you can achieve your individual goals.

MAKE THEM FEEL LIKE THEY MATTER

In my conversation with Ravinder, he spoke of something highlighted in many management books today: Employees want to know they matter, to be heard, and that the employer really cares about them. What better way to demonstrate this by educating your team to understand the goal setting process and helping them achieve their goals? You could take this to the next level (like Ravinder did) by finding other ways to be a part of this process. If someone wants to take a night class, you might adjust their work schedule. Let's say one of your employees is interested in a marketing career, why not let them help with your marketing needs? Look for opportunities to do the same for all your employees.

You want your employees to create a great experience for clientele? To motivate them to do so, you need to create a great experience of being an employee in your company. Make them raving fans of the company and they will make your customers raving fans of your company, as well.

Your assignment this week:

- Set up a team meeting just for the purpose of goal setting.
- Make up an agenda for the meeting to include goal setting and tracking. Include a bit of dream-building as many lose this as we get older.
- Look up SMART goals online or on my website.

You should have an annual team meeting just on this topic for all to share. They should be encouraged to share what goals they have achieved and to come up with new goals or to refine their current ones. You will change lives and one of those will be your own.

See you in the next productive week.

CHAPTER 23

WEEK 22—
PRODUCTIVITY

———

"Start with good people, lay out the rules, communicate with your employees, motivate them, and reward them. If you do all those things effectively, you can't miss."

—LEE IACOCCA

The one thing I would add to this advice: You need to track their productivity. This is a KPI that almost every business should know (see *Week 4—Knowing Your Numbers*). Whether it is a product, service, or sales that is the heart of your business, the productivity of your people should be tracked.

I was told many years ago that the average productivity rate in my industry was 72 percent and remains the same today! I learned that I could improve productivity just by sharing my team's statistics with them. To do this, I started with a simple chart on the employee bulletin board. It had the names of each employee at the bottom with the dollar amounts listed vertically. Every morning I would fill in the respective column for each employee's production from the prior day. It was a great success as my team was anxious to see the report every morning. Not only did they work at beating their own productivity, they started challenging each other. Tracking and reporting this attribute made a significant improvement in my productivity numbers and empowered my team. It became a game to them.

TRACK THE RIGHT THING

You, like many businesses, may be tracking efficiency, but productivity is the more important number to track. Productivity is about total production in a set amount of time. Efficiency is how fast a specific job is completed in a set amount of time. Bob may get a two-hour task done in the two hours allotted (100 percent efficient) but if that is all he has completed on an eight-hour shift, he is not very productive at 25 percent. Most businesses almost never get to 100 percent productivity (except a few of those in certain service businesses). Tracking your numbers is the first step. Figuring out the various causes of the lack of productivity is the second step, and the third is implementation of the solutions.

You can find more detailed information on how to calculate productivity and efficiency at this site: https://bit.ly/2fRuK75

WHAT'S CAUSING THE PROBLEM?

There are many causes for low productivity and these vary within every industry, but here are just a few that affect almost all industries (some of these are addressed in more detail in other chapters):

- Poor employee engagement: The Workplace Research Foundation reported that highly engaged employees were much more likely to have above-average productivity. A whopping 70 percent of employees do not feel they are engaged at work. Do you seek out feedback on any part of the business from your team? Do you do anything to show appreciation for your people and demonstrate that you are aware of the things they do for you? (See Weeks 8 & 21 about Teams)
- Work environment: What is the physical and physio-logical environment that your employees work in? Is everybody happy to work there, or do you have some employees that are upsetting the rest of the team? What is your mood when they are up or downbeat? How is

the lighting, furniture, cleanliness, and organization of the facilities? (See Week 18 - Cleaning the Business) I have seen many businesses that were so disorganized I wondered how they could keep any customers, let alone employees.

- Employee turnover: Any time you hire a new employee or terminate one, it affects the overall productivity on several fronts. It sidelines you from your existing team, takes extra time for them to work with the new team member, and affects morale, which affects productivity. (See Week 29 – Hiring)

- Internet and/or social media: What is your policy on this? (See Week 7 -Employee Handbook) Many, many hours are lost on this. You must have a strict policy for everyone to follow without being draconian.

- Stress, which leads to sick time off: What are the stress makers in your business? I have already mentioned a few. Others can be processes or lack thereof, inventory, deliveries, hours, equipment, and more.

- Improper or poor training: What happens when an employee is not properly trained? They seek out the guidance of their fellow employees, they may simply try to figure them out on their own (this slows them down) or wait for you to tell them how to do the task.

- No clear-cut goals or set expectations: If you were given a task without a definitive deadline or concrete goal to meet what would you do? I had one remodeler client whose team was not given concrete timelines to finish their projects so they usually took a day or two more than they should have. The owner made less money and the clients were upset by the delays.

- Lack of incentives to do more. Many are afraid to pay bonuses. But if business productivity increases by 10 percent, that increase goes directly to the bottom line, in most cases. So why not offer to share some of that profit with your team?

PEOPLE LOVE GAMES

In referring to my own story about tracking productivity: how can you turn this process into a game? Employee engagement can be enhanced if you can make a game out of this tracking, and competition can be a big motivator. Be sure to acknowledge their achievements in your meetings and reward them on their paycheck when they play the game well.

Your assignment this week:

- Determine what and how productivity should be tracked in your business.
- Determine what tools you need to track it (you may already have this in your company software programs).
- Determine what your goal is—keep this realistic.

- Determine how you will compensate/reward your employees for increases in productivity.
- Meet with your team(s) to share your ideas and ask for input for their engagement.

Keep the process as simple as possible to start. If properly introduced and set up, your team will find ways to help you enhance it.

Hope you are looking forward to next week's topic! It will be something to celebrate!

CHAPTER 24

WEEK 23—CELEBRATE YOUR CUSTOMER

"I have learned to imagine an invisible sign around each person's neck that says, 'Make me feel important!'

—MARY KAY ASH, FOUNDER, MARY KAY COSMETICS

There is a small restaurant chain in my area called Hobbee's. They have had a fiercely loyal customer following for years. They are not only happy to buy the company t-shirts, but they also love to have their photos taken while wearing them. Each of the stores has a large wall with photos of their customers taken from every corner of the earth in which they are wearing the restaurant's t-shirts. Customers spend time reviewing the photos to see who they know and if they have been to any of the places that others have visited. And in turn, they bring in photos of themselves to add to the collection. Of course, the company's social media sites have these photos posted as well, which generates many, many likes. Why is this such a popular thing? Because who doesn't like to see a picture of themselves? We all do. Look at the explosion of selfies on the internet. As I have mentioned in other chapters, people like to be a part of like-minded groups and be celebrated by a brand they love and care about.

A PICTURE IS WORTH 1,000 WORDS

I have seen other businesses do the same or similar sort of thing. I remember visiting a small local coffee shop that had a large collection of coffee mugs hanging on the wall, each with the name of a regular customer. And then there was a story I heard about an auto repair shop that had established a *"High Mileage Club."* They had three different photo collections on a wall in their customer waiting area: 100,000 miles, 200,000 miles and the *"Over 300,000 miles"* sections. The wall was covered with pictures of smiling customers and their high mileage vehicles. This idea not only generated repeat business but was a silent testimonial to new customers on how well the shop was at taking care of its customers' vehicles.

KEEP THEM COMING BACK FOR MORE

Many businesses use some sort of loyalty system to keep customers coming back other than just a follow-up program (see Week 43 - Know Your Customer). I was in a small coffee shop recently that gave me a loyalty card with my change. It had a *"buy 10 get 1 free"* deal that already had two punches on it even though I had only purchased one coffee. I was very tempted to keep the card and make plans to return (the coffee was very good) even though the likelihood of my returning soon was quite low, as I was a long way from home.

ALMOST EVERYONE LOVES COFFEE

Umpqua Bank has a very interesting loyalty program: free coffee and a place to take a break. The company's branches are quite different from all other banks (though some of their competitors are coming up with similar concepts). What you will find is a coffee station with freshly brewed coffee, the day's local paper, and some comfy chairs to sit in while reading the paper. If you like, you can take home some of their own blend of coffee beans to enjoy later. They have many regulars who come by just to visit. They do welcome prospective customers to take advantage of their hospitality, as well.

What ideas can you think of to increase the likelihood of your customer coming back more often and remaining loyal? Remember, it is always less expensive to keep a customer than to get a new one. Keep this in mind as well: Your competitors are working hard to get your customers to become their customers.

Here are some ideas to consider (more are on the website):

- Loyalty cards—buy X get X free but give two points to start with.
- Discount coupons or no charge extras for achieving X level of purchases.
- Photos of happy customers—on wall of business, social media, newsletters, etc.
- Customer appreciation—open house night/day, BBQs, customer education seminars/workshops, thank you cards/notifications
- Birthday/anniversary cards and/or gifts.
- Best customer survey—not a Google or Yelp review—this sent out specially, will make the customer feel special and will help you get some valuable info (see www.1week1thing.com for forms).
- Referral bonuses—dining out cards, free car wash/detail, etc. for referring clients.
- Award drawings—ticket for every purchase, drawing held quarterly or annually.

HOST AN EVENT

Every October the CSR Real Estate Services hosts an event called the Annual Pumpkin Patch. They invite all their clients to bring their kids to enjoy face painting, crafts, a petting zoo, pumpkins, and a costume parade and contest for both children and adults. They also have appetizers and champagne (for the adults). I have been to a few of the open house events at their headquarters and can personally attest that they put on great events.

They do many other customer friendly events. For example, they host free seminars to help students and their parents with college planning. The message here is that they know how to show appreciation to their clientele and the community.

People like to do business with people they know, like, and trust. People are very tribal, which means that once they feel like you are part of their tribe or they are a part of your tribe, it is very unlikely the competition can take them away from you even if offered a lower price!

What sort of events do you host to show appreciation for your customers? This could be for all your clientele or just VIPs. Look to other owners that are good promoters in your area for advice on how to proceed.

Here is a list of some ideas:

- Open house party: It can be as simple as a BBQ or as elaborate as a catered party at a venue away from your place of business.
- Educational night/lunch/breakfast/workshop: Help your clientele (and prospects) with some basic education for themselves and more about what you offer. If you are an attorney, share some insights on your area of law. If you are a chef, maybe you can share some good eating habits, cooking tips, etc. Many of the top auto repair shops I have worked with have hosted *"women's auto care nights"* where they educate women about the basics of car maintenance. You could also sponsor an event not related to your business, like CSR does with college planning. Bring in a guest speaker on a topic of interest to your clientele.
- Sponsor a Chamber event: It's good for your clientele to network with other business folk. A local Workers Comp walk-in clinic did this a few years ago. They invited all their clients and vendors to attend the event. Everyone had a great time and lots of new connections were made. The event was one of the best I have attended and was a topic of conversation for many weeks afterward.
- Organize a trip: It can be to a winery, the theater, ball game (our local AA baseball team is a favorite for this kind of activity) or some other event. These events are

usually low cost but high value with many happy to pay something to be there. (Employees love these sorts of events also, but you should foot the bill for the employee outings.)

Your assignment this week:

- Choose and implement (or update) at least one of these strategies.
- Schedule the appropriate time (as needed) for planning and implementation of any event you might choose to host.
- Start by looking at what others are doing in your industry.
- Add to the list of ideas in this chapter by writing down everything that comes to mind no matter how silly, outrageous, or costly, just do it.
- Enlist your team to help and don't be afraid to seek out professional help.

The more you celebrate your customers, the more loyal and appreciative they will be to you and your business, and the more likely they'll refer others to you.

Make sure you complete this exercise annually to plan your activities and event(s). Make it a habit. You will enjoy these events, as will your clientele.

Believe me when I tell you next week will be different.

CHAPTER 25

WEEK 24—BELIEFS AND VALUES—ARE THEY HOLDING YOU BACK?

———

My wife has a favorite saying: *"Be careful of what you want to believe or have to believe."*

Mark Gunnerson was a sales representative selling a new form of automotive repair shop information—on CD-ROM. Before the advent of this CD-ROM system, all repair information was in book form and took up loads of space in a shop. Since CD-ROM was a cutting-edge system, the cost of access was quite high for the time but was revolutionary and quite profitable to use. Because the cost was high, his belief was that only the best shops in the best part of town would be his prospects. That all changed one day when his manager asked why he was not calling on the shops in the poorer parts of his region and challenged him to foray into those areas. One of his first calls netted him a sale. Not only did his product help the shop make a lot more money, but it also changed his attitude and beliefs about who was a good prospect. And he changed the beliefs of his customer who had a similar belief about his own clients—the owner did not believe the system would work with his clientele. The change of their beliefs started with a challenge (Mark's manager), followed by a leap of faith (action—calling on a new area), that created a new belief (who would be a good client).

OUR BELIEFS CONTROL US

Everyone has beliefs and values that control how we respond to life. They affect our actions and interactions with people, as we saw in the story about Mark and his customer. This book may challenge some of your beliefs that hopefully will have an affect on how you run your business.

Our beliefs start to be formed from our earliest age by how our parents talked to us and how we were treated by them and others in our daily lives. Those beliefs affect our values and how we operate our lives in relationship to those beliefs.

What if your parents said something like, *"Those rich people only got that way because they stole from others or cheated on their taxes."*? One of your beliefs might be that all rich people are bad. If you had this belief and some of your values are integrity and honesty, then having a lot of money might be difficult. If you were in sales, asking for a lot of money might be a challenge.

What if your parents told you things like, *"The sky's the limit. You can achieve anything!"* or, *"Work hard and you can go far,"* or *"Always be ready to help another—you never know when that will come back to help you later in life,"* or *"Readers are leaders"*? How different would your beliefs be, and how would they affect your values and actions?

Even as adults, we are still being affected by what people say to us, but our core beliefs and values are what drives our actions. Another person who is very close to you and has immense influence: you. We talk to ourselves more than anyone else and say things to ourselves that we would not say to others. Our beliefs come out when we say things like, *"I can't be rich"*, *"I could never learn another language,"* *"I don't have the body type to run a marathon,"* and more. These are very self-limiting and destructive, but you can change them like Mark changed his beliefs about certain prospective customers. Change is the operative word here.

- Be aware of the things you tell yourself. Take a good listen at the things you are saying. If they are negative find better statements.

- Write down some of the things you tell yourself. This will help you figure out just what beliefs you have, and it will also help you to find ways to change them. Knowledge is power.

- When you hear yourself say, *"I can't_____,"* stop and ask yourself, why not? Change all the *"I can'ts"* to *"How do I _____?"*

- Take a beliefs and values test. From the results of these tests, you can determine which of these beliefs or values may be holding you back and which are helping. You will probably find that your values and your company's are much the same.

- Research online—there are many other ways to determine your beliefs and values. Go to www.1week1thing.com for more links.

- Read books and listen to the many recordings available about beliefs and values. There is a wealth of information out there to help you.

Your assignment this week:

- Find a workshop/seminar/webinar on the subject and sign up for it.
- Take a beliefs and values test. Here is one at https://bit.ly/2XmiE4X
- You may want to retake the test, or better yet, take a different one the following year. You can never learn too much about yourself.

As I mentioned earlier, your beliefs started forming the day you were born so don't expect to be making great changes immediately. It will take time and effort to learn about your beliefs and how to change or adapt them to get the results you want in life. But the effort will pay off handsomely in your life and business!

Up next week: another small thing that can get you big results.

CHAPTER 26

WEEK 25—THE LOWLY POST-IT NOTE

———

"Let me tell you something big: give importance to little things!"

— MEHMET MURAT ILDAN

Larry was a very successful business owner. One thing about Larry: He was a prodigious marketer. He has read many books on the topic and was always open to trying new ideas. He was also an extraordinary tracker of all his business activities. From advertising to work-flow, he tracked it all. One of his marketing tools was a standard sized Post-it Note with his company logo and phone number. They are an inexpensive marketing tool. He gave them to all his customers and to just about everyone he met at the many networking and Civic events he attended. Who couldn't use more Post-its?

After many years of being a renter and losing one lease after another, he was finally able to purchase his own building. It was not a simple solution to finding a permanent location for the business, but luckily the new building was close to his last location.

Ah, but he had some serious remodeling to do. His new place was not laid out for an automotive repair shop, and it would take many months and many more dollars before he could begin operating out of the new location. One of the biggest hurdles was getting his building plans approved by the city planning department. This was one of the biggest delays in getting things started.

IT WAS A SMALL THING

Well, the day comes for Larry to submit his plans to the planning department. The clerk reviews the drawings and documents and thanks Larry for them. He tells Larry that it will be several weeks before he can get an answer on their decision, as there were many other submitted plans already in the queue. The clerk grabs a Post-it off his desk, sticks one on Larry's plans, makes a note and places the plans near the bottom of a stack of others. Larry notices that the Post-it is his and mentions this to the clerk. The clerk responds, *"Oh, you are that Larry? Well, I will have to see if I can get this expedited for you!"* and proceeds to move the plans to the top of the stack!

Now it wasn't just the Post-it note that made the difference in this case, it was Larry's image in his community as it was portrayed through many activities and other marketing. Larry is an active member of the local Chamber of Commerce. He and his wife have been honored with many local business awards. But the lowly Post-it helped make the connection a successful one.

10 X 10 STRATEGY

Good marketers have at least ten different strategies in ten different places going on at any one time. It could be something as large as a billboard or as little as a Post-it. The secret to any marketing is making sure it will catch the attention of your target audience. When I ran my own shop, I was always looking for those items to hand out to customers and prospects, like Post-it notes, that they would use often or see on places like their refrigerator (think magnetic calendar or local youth ball team schedule). I wanted my business name to be present even subliminally, so every time they had a need for my services, my business came to mind.

What sort of things might work for your business? Keep in mind that not everything will work, but you won't know if you don't try. Some things might not work now or ever, or they might do so in the future as markets and marketing change. Be adventurous and creative. Avoid allowing your ego to get involved. A billboard with a picture of you may not bring them in, unless you are already famous or lucky enough to be very good looking! Anything on your list that is tied to a time of year? Plan and schedule any orders or arrangements needed so you can be prepared to launch the campaign on time. For example, if you are planning to hand out custom calendars to your clients, be sure to have them ready before the new year. To make sure you are investing your dollars wisely, you need to track where your business is coming from. (You should have gotten this message from previous chapters.)

Your assignment this week:

- Make a list of the new things/strategies that might work to market your business. (A large list available at www.1week1thing.com)
- Review your current marketing budget to see how much you have to spend.
- Schedule a campaign and/or order any promotional items on your list.

- Review this list of items and update, add, delete, etc. at least annually.

Keep it simple and fun. And don't count out that lowly Post-it!

See you next week when we look at the best things . . . and the worst.

CHAPTER 27

WEEK 26—WHAT ARE YOU BEST AT?

———

"The good-to-great companies did not focus principally on what to do to become great; they focused equally on what not to do and what to stop doing."

— JAMES C. COLLINS, *GOOD TO GREAT*

In his book, *Good to Great,* Jim Collins tells the story of Kimberly-Clark and how they made a phenomenal change in what they were doing—they sold their paper mills, the core of what they were known for over 100 years. Why did they do this? Because they were highly successful in developing the Kleenex brand and realized they could do so much better in the consumer business versus the coated paper business, which was mostly sold to magazine companies. The consumer business fit the *"Three Circles"* test (see below). Against all outside opinion, they sold their mills and focused on what they could be best in the world at. Twenty-five years later, Kimberly-Clark emerged from the fray as the No. 1 paper-based consumer products company in the world, outperforming many other companies in many ways, including stock valuation.[25]

STOP DOING THAT!

This all comes down to disciplined action: the *"Stop Doing"* list. What is it that your business, like Kimberly-Clark, should stop doing?

In the book *Good to Great*, Jim Collins talks about the *"Hedgehog"* concept and *"Three Circles"* test. Here is an excerpt from the book to explain the two ideas:

Are you a hedgehog or a fox? In his famous essay *"The Hedgehog and the Fox,"* Isaiah Berlin divided the world into hedgehogs and foxes, based upon an ancient Greek parable: *"The fox knows many things, but the hedgehog knows one big thing."*

---

30 Jim Collins, *Good to Great* - Articles: Stop Doing That. https://bit.ly/2MpBAj6

Those who built the good-to-great companies were, to one degree or another, hedgehogs. They used their hedgehog nature to drive toward what we came to call a Hedgehog Concept for their companies. Those who led the comparison companies tended to be foxes, never gaining the clarifying advantage of a Hedgehog Concept, being instead scattered, diffused, and inconsistent. company logo and phone number. They are an inexpensive marketing tool. He gave them to all his customers and

Three Circles of the Hedgehog Concept

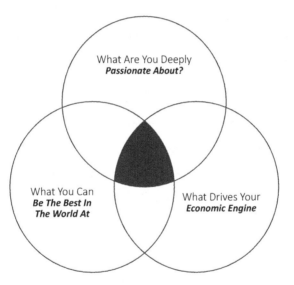

I know of many businesses that get excited about expanding their product and/or service offerings only to end up with a lot more business, but not any more profit. The expansion dilutes the focus and requires extra energy to handle all the

dissimilar programs. I must admit that I did a lot of the same thing when running my businesses. But I learned to stop doing work that the business was not really equipped to handle effectively. In the last several years, I have received offers to help start other enterprises with the promise of more income. But if I measure any of those offers with the three circles, they all fall outside of what I am best at.

WHAT MIGHT YOU ONLY DO?

There are a lot of examples of businesses I know that are very focused on what they do and are diligent not to take on something outside of their three circles.

- The concrete contractor who did my sidewalks and driveway doesn't do any asphalt or pavers.
- The homebuilders and remodelers that don't do any commercial projects and the commercial contractors don't do homes.
- The BMW repair shop that won't fix your Mercedes even though it just broke down in their parking lot.
- The attorney that only does employment law for businesses or the other employment law attorney that only works with employees.
- The restaurant that only does breakfast and lunch or one type of food, like Japanese.

- A re-manufacturer that is an expert with only one brand or type of product.

There are so many advantages of having a laser-like focus on what you do. You will find it is easier to staff and manage your team(s). If you need special tooling, machines, equipment, supplies, facilities, etc. the focus can save you time and money, not to mention that it is a poor investment to have anything you don't use to capacity. Imagine purchasing a software program for hundreds of dollars only to use it occasionally and for only one small part of your business activities.

A few ways to determine what you should stop doing:

- What takes more time to do than most other things you are doing?
- What are the least profitable things you are doing?
- What is it that creates the most turmoil in your business? (employee dissatisfaction/turnover/injuries, customer dissatisfaction, frustration on your part, quality control issues, etc.)
- What is a sideline product/service that you took on to make just a bit more money but doesn't really fit the three circles?

Your assignment this week:

- Answer the three questions:
    - *"What can you be the best in the world at?"*
    - *"What drives your economic engine?"*
    - *"What are you passionate about?"* (should be easy to answer—this was in the very first week.)
- Meet with your team(s) to review these questions and the things you should not be doing.
- Determine what you are going to stop doing.
- Check with your team(s) at least once a year to see if you are still on track and not doing something you should not be doing.

It might be daunting and a bit scary to stop doing certain things but doing so will make what you should only be doing so much better and more profitable.

See you next week when we talk about how to make more money. That should be fun!

CHAPTER 28

WEEK 27—INCREASE YOUR AVERAGE SALE

———

"Every accomplishment starts with the decision to try."

—UNKNOWN

"For more than 40 years, Walgreens was no more than an average company, tracking the general market. Then in 1975 out of the blue, Walgreens' stock began to climb. And climb. And climb. It just kept climbing. From December 31, 1975, to January 1, 2000, $1 invested in Walgreens beat $1 invested in Intel by nearly two times, General Electric by nearly five times,

and Coca-Cola by nearly eight times. It beat the general stock market by more than 15 times." [26]

Just how did Walgreens do it? They did a few simple things: They decided to get out of the restaurant business (they had food counters in their stores for generations), worked on attracting higher paying clientele, and increase the average sales amount to each customer. They focused on giving more and getting more from their existing clientele instead of spending more to get more customers. And it worked wonderfully!

IT'S NOT MORE CUSTOMERS, BUT MORE
FROM EACH CUSTOMER THAT YOU WANT

Many of the businesses I have worked with are mostly concerned with how to get more people to come to them. Depending on the type of business you are in, this may be your biggest need. But I find that many are leaving money on the table and doing a disservice to their existing clientele. What most businesses need is to focus on how to maximize the average sale amount—one of the key numbers I mentioned in the *"Know Your Numbers"* chapter.

---

326 ollins, *Good to Great* - Articles: How Change Doesn't Happen
   https://bit.ly/2MpBAj6

You could just raise your prices (see Week 32 *"Raise Your Prices"*), but that is not always the answer or feasible. What you need to do is look for all the things that you can do or sell to a customer that they may need or want. Ever find out sometime after a customer visits that they bought something you sell from someone else? The goal is not to encourage overselling, but to make sure the customer gets all their needs covered in a one-stop transaction that just happens to be at your business.

SIMPLE STEPS TO INCREASES

Remember the McDonald's phrase you have undoubtedly heard many times, *"Would you like fries with that?"* Increasing the average sale might be as simple as asking for the additional sale. *"Is there anything else I can help you with today?"*

Maybe it's time to modify or add to your talk tracks or add other tactics to increase your average sale:

- If you are in a service business, are there any additional services you provide that the customer may need or want, but you are not offering because they only asked for the one thing?
- If you are in a product business, what items can you suggest to go with the one(s) that they just purchased? If you

sell gourmet coffees and you sell tea as well, why not ask the customer if they happen to drink tea?

- If you are in the restaurant business, is your team using the McDonald's tactic? If not, why not? Maybe they need some training to sell more desserts, coffee, and the nicer bottles of wine. At the end of the meal the server might ask, *"And what sort of dessert are you thinking of to go with a nice cup of coffee or tea?"*

- There was a printer in my area that got tired of hearing people say, *"Gee, I didn't know you did that!"* so he made up a flier with that title and listed all the services he offered. It greatly increased his average sale, and his customers were happy with being able to get more done in one place.

- How about a checklist for the customer to fill out when they come to your place of business? This survey or form might prompt them to ask you for something they may have forgotten.

Training your team and setting goals is key to accomplishing increased average sales. This is covered in several chapters of this book.

Your assignment for this week:

- Find out what is your average sale amount (if you don't know already).

- Create a process on how to increase the amount.
- Ask your team if they ask for additional sales but are not getting them often enough. This is a conversion issue and may be a call for some sales training, as well.
- Make up a list of all the items you want to sell more of, and work with your team to increase the focus.
- What higher margin products and/or services can you sell more of?
- Review this process on at least an annual basis.

You already have the customer in your business. People's purchases are usually motivated by convenience and quality over price. Keep this in mind as you build your strategy to increase your average sale amount.

See you next week when we talk more about the little things in your business.

CHAPTER 29

WEEK 28—IT'S THE LITTLE THINGS THAT ARE REALLY BIG THINGS

My personal tagline on my email: *"The difference between success and failure is quite small. It is the seemingly small things that you do or don't do that make the difference."*

At the beginning of many of the seminars and workshops that I lead, I ask the attendees, *"What is the difference between success and failure?"* I then hold up my thumb and forefinger very, very close to each other, but not together, and say "About this much!" And then I make the above statement.

THE LITTLE CHANGES

Jeff, a longtime friend, used to run a high-tech engineering firm. He was a great employer and very nice fellow. Every six to eight months he would change something in the offices. He would replace all the trash cans. Or he gave the employees new desk accessories, such as staplers. One Christmas, he gave everyone a new desk chair (not such a small thing). What effect did this have on the employees? They felt special and appreciated. Morale was kept high and turnover low. He started doing this at the suggestion of his partner, even though he was skeptical at first.

Maybe my friend's partner had heard of a study that was done to see just what things would enhance employee productivity. The researchers tried different colors of paint. They changed the lighting and many other aspects of the work environment. Every time they made any change, productivity jumped, and employee morale improved. But a while after the change, productivity would slip until they made another change. In the end they found the reason for improvement was that the employees felt the changes were made just for them, so they felt appreciated and were happier. Quite simple.

THE LITTLE THINGS HAVE A BIG EFFECT

In Week 18 - Clean the Business, I talked about how cleaning the business, a big thing, can help attract and keep customers, as well as affect your employees. But this chapter is about the small things you can do to affect you, your team and your clients. The things that don't cost much time, effort, or money.

What kind of small things, you ask? Some things may be obvious while others are not so much, and you may or may not be doing some already. Here are some things to consider for the team:

- Thank them for a job well done. You'd be surprised how few bosses ever offer a simple *"thanks"* and encouragements.
- Surprise baked goods, lunch, or other treats.
- Change of uniforms (if you use them).
- New anything in your place of business now and then
- Surprise gift cards for exceptional service to a customer (catch them in the act of excellence—no matter how small).
- Brag to your clientele about your team members (make sure they are in earshot when you do this).
- Celebrate their special days (b-days, anniversaries, tenure, etc.) with the team.
- Ask about their goals to date (See Week 21).
- Get them out of the business early some day!
- Take them on an offsite excursion.
- Make sure the employee restroom is as clean as the customer restroom.

Wowing the customer is covered in Week 19, but here are a few additional small things to consider for your clientele:

- Fresh custom coffee in the waiting area. (No coffee? how about a $5 gift card to the coffee shop nearby?)
- A mini chocolate bar with their purchase (EG: Ghirardelli minis).
- Dog treats – if they have one, but ask first
- Thank you card with a very nice restaurant gift card for that big referral.
- Fresh flowers for the ladies.
- Gift packaged quality pen (not the $2 imprinted ones normally given).
- Something unexpected included with their purchase.

Your assignment this week:

- Determine what small thing you want to do this week for your team.
- Determine what small thing you want to do this week for you clientele.
- Make a list of small things you want to do in the future and book them into your calendar.
- In life and business, it all comes down to the small things that can affect your business in big ways.

Thought this chapter was big? Wait until you read next week's!

CHAPTER 30

WEEK 29—YOUR HIRING PROCESS

———

"People are not your most important asset. The right people are."

—JIM COLLINS, AUTHOR OF *GOOD TO GREAT*

The job candidate has made it through the second and final interviews prior to the background check and TB tests. What follows next is the acceptance of the compensation package. The candidate knows the salary offered by the company (like most companies, this one wants to underpay the market) but is still interested as the company has made a contingent offer or provide other benefits over more money. They are still thinking about it. But most will walk away if the company will not negotiate up on the salary. And this after so many weeks to find the right person.

HAVE PATIENCE

This process is what Jaime Orendac, OHR of MyOHR, LLC, goes through for companies all the time. She says, *"Finding the right people is a process that is challenging, [and] takes time and patience."* To get the one candidate it will take finding five finalists. To find those five, it will take fifteen to twenty good candidates. To find the fifteen to twenty you will need to have sixty to eighty prospects that fit your requirements out of all the responses to your job posting. A daunting process, but you must keep it moving to find the one you want. This process includes the phone interviews and face-to-face interviews with the most likely candidates. The time frame to do all this? It is usually four to eight weeks.

Those of us who have any experience in hiring have made the mistake of hiring the wrong person because we were desperate to fill a vacant spot or too busy to take the time to look for the right people. Later we regret doing so, firing that individual (or they leave because they were not happy, etc.) and we start the process all over again. This process costs lots of money and time spent in orientation and training. I repeat this phrase to my clients all the time: Hire slow and fire fast.

USE A PROCESS

This process should be used no matter what the economic climate may be. At the time I am writing this book, we are experiencing the lowest unemployment rates in history. Every company is scrambling for employees. Some industries, such as the trades, are seeing declining numbers of available candidates. The thinning list of candidates leads to higher rates of poaching as well. No matter what the current status, you need to work hard and use the process to find the right people.

There are several different hiring processes I have heard of and used myself (see them on www.1week.1thing.com) but the good ones have approximately the same process. You can do this yourself or hire others, like Jaime, to do this for you. Or consider a recruiter to find some candidates and pre-screen them for you.

- Write the job description (see Week 6 *"HR Manual"*). An in-house HR professional or hired expert does this for you.
- Write the ad for posting. This is where you place your bait to catch the ones you are looking for. *"Men wanted for hazardous journey to the South Pole. Small wages, bitter cold, long months of complete darkness, constant danger. Safe return doubtful. Honor and recognition in case of success."* Supposedly written by Shackleton seeking sailors

for his trip to Antarctica. The point is how can you make an ad that will be that tantalizing and different from all others seeking the same people.

- Use a funnel or sieve process that will separate out those that don't qualify early in the process. Could be a few simple questions or instructions on what the next step is. It's amazing how many will sort themselves out of the process when asked to take a next step.
- Use phone interviews to do more sorting. Have a list of key questions. Get help from your HR resource(s) to make sure you are not asking something not allowed by law.
- Next step is the face-to-face interviews. Some processes suggest group interviews and/or team-included interviews. The group interview can be especially beneficial if the new hire's success is dependent on buy-in of other key players or direct reports with key knowledge.
- Once your candidate is a finalist and the negotiations are complete, they have passed the TB and background checks (there are companies that do this for reasonable rates) you send a final offer letter for their acceptance.

They accept, and you are done! But wait, there is more! Next is the on-boarding process, but that is covered in Weeks 6 & 7 - HR and Employee Handbooks sections. My point here is to make sure they are properly brought aboard. I have seen too many people get hired only to see them leave a few weeks later because they were just thrown into their place and left to do their job without any oversight or training. Please do not manage by default as Michael Gerber talks about in his book, *The E-Myth*.

Your assignment this week:

- Whether you are actively seeking staff or not, review your hiring process and see where and what you need to make changes to what you are doing now.
- Since most businesses tend to have openings on a regular basis, consider keeping a job posting on the job boards all the time. Considering how many suspects it takes to find that one great candidate, it's not a bad idea to keep looking.
- Make sure you have a Careers/Jobs tab on your website with a link to an application available all the time.
- Think about your team members. Who might be retiring soon or may be getting to the point where they have grown so much that they may be thinking of leaving for a place with new opportunities? Make plans to be ready to fill their spot when the time comes.

Hiring is one of the most challenging things for most business owners. Proper planning and processes in place can reduce the stress of hiring and help in keeping employees for a longer duration.

Up next week: something that is mutually beneficial and profitable.

CHAPTER 31

WEEK 30—MUTUAL MARKETING

—

"Just one great partnership with the right person can have an incredible impact on your business success."

—JANIONI OGG AND JO FOSTER

Brandy owned a women's clothing store. She was always jealous of the salon across the street. Not only were they busy but had the type of clientele she wanted more of. One day she approached the owner of the salon with a proposal. She recently obtained a large quantity of kimonos for about $9 each. She offered to give one to each of the salon's clients at no cost to the salon. All she asked for in return was the salon's client list. She would foot the bill to send a card to each client on behalf of the salon stating that, in appreciation for being a good client of the salon, they would get a free kimono at the clothing store across the street. All they needed to do was bring in the card to get the kimono. The promotion was a great success as many of the women who came for their free kimono browsed the store and bought something else. This was a win-win for both businesses—Brandy got more new clients for a low investment and the salon's clients were more loyal than ever because of the "*free*" gift. This was true for those that did not redeem the card, as well.

WHO CAN YOU PARTNER WITH?

What business in your area has the same or similar clientele to yours? What can you offer to that clientele to get them to come to your business? How can you market another business to your customers in exchange for them marketing to your business? We've all been to a business that has at least one business card on their front counter that belongs to another business. This a good way to mutual market, but not great. You need to have something a bit more direct, one that will get the phone to ring or get the prospect to come to you.

One question that you may need to answer first: Just who is your ideal client? If you know this, it will be a lot easier to 'share' customers with a mutual marketing partner. (You should have completed this exercise in Week 5.)

Here are a few suggestions other than the one that Brandy used:

- Go to a local popular restaurant and ask for a deal on gift cards—such as $75 for $100 card. Tell them you are going to use them as thank you gifts for business and/or referrals from your clientele and that you will be marketing this to all your customers. Ask if they would display your business card in their customer waiting area, as well.
- Offer to advertise a local business on coupons with every receipt. Ask them if they would do the same for you or how much they would be willing to pay for you to do this for them. A few good examples:
  - the tailor/clothing store and a dry cleaner
  - the auto repair shop and a car wash/detail shop
  - the used/new car dealer and an insurance agent or a banker
  - the home remodeler and an insurance agent
  - tax attorney and accountant
  - employment lawyer and an HR professional
- Offer to put your logo on something the business uses every day and allow them to use a similar tactic at your business
  - The tray liner the food is served on at many casual diners
  - The paper coffee cup insulator

Your assignment this week:

- Make a list of all the businesses that deal with the same type of clientele as you do. Contact the business(es) with an offer to do some mutual marketing.
- Do this exercise on an annual basis, if not more often, as all marketing grows stale and you need to find new prospects from different sources.

Need more ideas? More ideas online at www.1week1thing. com

Next week's topic will benefit you in many ways.

CHAPTER 32

WEEK 31—BENEFITS— ADDING VALUE TO YOUR TEAM

"The way your employees feel is the way your customers will feel. And if your employees don't feel valued, neither will your customers."

—SYBIL F. STERSHIC, AUTHOR OF *TAKING CARE OF THE PEOPLE WHO MATTER MOST: A GUIDE TO EMPLOYEE-CUSTOMER CARE*

In any economy, finding and keeping great employees is always a challenge. And it is not always money alone that motivates and keeps employees happy. Making them feel appreciated, encouraged, and recognized is very important. But another way to make them feel valued is to offer them benefits in addition to and/or in lieu of pay raises. Several of my clients have lost employees and potential employees because they do not offer any benefits.

IT'S NOT ALL ABOUT MONEY

A 2017 study by the SCORE group reports that benefits and perks in the workplace are often more important to employees than higher pay.[27] Recent research from Glassdoor found that more than half (57 percent) of people said benefits and perks are among their top considerations before accepting a job, and four in five workers say they would prefer new benefits over a pay raise.

BENEFITS MAY BE CHEAPER THAN RAISES—FOR BOTH OF YOU.

Consider how much more an employee would have to make to get health or other benefits on their own. You, as the employer, would have to pay more in taxes and Workers Comp insurance on the higher wages they would seek. Providing benefits in lieu of pay increases would be more

---

32 BioSpace, What's More Important at Work: Better Perks and Benefits or Higher Salary (Blog) https://bit.ly/31sXExb (June 27, 2018)

beneficial to both you and the employee. And you will get a happier, more motivated, and more loyal employee.

According to a recent article in Fast Company magazine, these are the top five benefits employees are most interested in:

1. Health care insurance (e.g., medical, dental): 40 percent
2. Vacation/paid time off: 37 percent
3. Performance bonus: 35 percent
4. Paid sick days: 32 percent
5. 401(k) plan, retirement plan, and/or pension: 31 percent

But there are many, many more.

- Ancillary insurance (Aflac, life insurance, disability, etc.)
- Flexible hours
- Carpool/commuter perks
- Profit-sharing
- Company sponsored events
- Casual office days
- Equipment/tool allowances (for trades people)
- Family leave
- Student loan aid
- Educational classes tuition assistance/Professional development
- Time off to vote

- Gym membership
- Snacks provided
- Financial planning assistance
- ID/fraud protection
- Pet at the office day
- Volunteer days off
- Health Savings Accounts
- Discounts on major attractions and travel

Depending on the makeup of your personnel, some benefits will be more desirable than others. One more thing about the benefits: not all need to be paid for by you. Many benefits can be perks like discounts on products or services they could not get on their own. Many businesses offer to pay a portion of things like health insurance.

If you don't have a good benefits broker, ask your HR or payroll professional for references. They tend to work well together and are a good resource for you.

Your assignment this week:

- Review what benefits you provide, if any.
- Look at the lists provided. See any that you can offer?
- Ask some of your key employees for suggestions.
- Seek out your peers in your industry to see what they are providing and how well those are working for them.

- Then go shopping for the best provider and implement the benefit.

Your employees will love it and your bottom line should improve by the increased productivity and employee longevity.

Up next week: more talk about money.

CHAPTER 33

WEEK 32—RAISE YOUR PRICES—REGULARLY

"What I 'charge' today has nothing to do with yesterday or tomorrow. It has to do with 'now!'"

— DAVID WAYNE WILSON [PRICING NEWS DAILY, 2014]

It was in the news today: San Jose Water District asks the PUC permission to raise its rates another 7 percent. I pay almost three times as much for water as I did ten years ago. As I write this book, I have received three letters in the last two weeks from subscription services that, due to increased costs of doing business, will be raising their rates. My satellite bill went up 30 percent this month. They cited increased costs from the content providers. The price of gasoline increased by almost a dollar in the last three months! What costs have not gone up substantially for the consumer in the last few years?

And as a business, I am confident that you have seen many of your costs increased along with new fees levied by your local and state governments. Your labor costs and those related to those costs have gone up. What about any equipment you may have purchased, updated, or must replace? Your utilities, insurance, rent, and more have all gone up.

WHEN DID YOU LAST RAISE YOUR PRICES?

With everything else increasing, how about the prices you charge for your services and/or products? When was the last time you raised them? If you are like many business owners I speak to, you have not done so in some time. You are not alone. Remember my earlier story about Bruce not raising his prices for five years? One of my favorite Italian restaurants was just like that, but finally raised their prices and changed some items from being included with a meal to a charged item. And I was the one who suggested they do so—because I wanted them to stay in business!

Why do so many business owners not raise their rates? Fear! Fear of losing customers. Instead of raising their prices, many will try to reduce their operating costs wherever they can (marketing is usually one of the first to go—a VERY bad idea) to make up for the loss of income. Or they reduce staff, services, or quality, which in the long run reduces customer satisfaction, which eventually causes the business to close or the owner to work for meager wages. Not a pretty picture. If you have a very loyal clientele who you offer great services to and create a great experience for, raising your prices on a regular basis will not result in lost clientele.

For every business I have helped to increase their prices, they did not go out of business; they stayed in business and thrived. The increases were applied gradually, and no one complained. If you are already giving exceptional service, great value, and have happy customers, the increases should not be a big issue. Another plus of raising your rates is that it will weed out the bargain hunters. Raising your rates by 10 percent will more than make up for any loss of customers that may happen (see discounting vs. increasing prices chart at www.1week1thing.com.)

HOW MUCH TO INCREASE?

You should be tracking your numbers by now (if you have read Week 4 - Know Your Numbers) so you should be noticing a slippage of profits if you haven't raised your rates. Many businesses set up a time each quarter to raise the rates accordingly, while others raise their prices as the increases are passed on to them—the gas stations do this regularly.

This method will not be so noticeable to your clientele—unless you are in the gasoline business because you must post it. And don't be swayed by whatever CPI percentage is being touted by the government. Just look at your fixed operating costs year over year to get a good picture of what the real percentage of your increased costs. The CPI numbers are manipulated regularly.

WHAT TO TELL YOUR CUSTOMER

When asked why prices have increased, be sure to give good answers other than the fact that you want more profits. Share with your clientele any new laws such as minimum wage increases, new regulations that require new equipment, or local tax levies. Typically, people will not be happy about these things but understand when told truthfully about them. We all know prices are going up on everything—it is a part of life.

Your assignment this week:

- Make a schedule of when and how much you need to raise your rates/prices to maintain your margins and attain your profit goals.
- Set to review this on an annual basis and adjust as needed.

Stick to your goals and plans so you will be able to continue to operate a profitable business.

See you next week: it's all about giving.

CHAPTER 34

WEEK 33—GIVE BACK

———

"We make a living by what we get. We make a life by what we give."

—WINSTON S. CHURCHILL

Stockton, Calif., is in the heart of the San Joaquin Valley, alongside the delta. It has been a hub for local agriculture and shipping due to its location. It has also been the hub for many gangs for the same reason. Due to this, the town has suffered a bad reputation for violence and poverty. About ten years ago, Stockton went bankrupt but has since recovered. Like many cities, it is not all bad and there are many nice spots in town. But the bad reputation had persisted until Bob and his friends decided to take action.

Bob Melrose, a partner in a local business, Brookside Optometric Group, was fed up with all the complaining by many locals about how bad the town was. He felt that "We should not just stand by and listen to others complain." Bob is a man of action. He, his partners, and few other business leaders in town decided they were going to do their best to change some attitudes. They started buying tickets to local shows and events. They encouraged others to experience the town, as well. Today Stockton has many wonderful events, venues, and places to dine that draw many from the surrounding areas. They even have three minor league (just one step below the majors) sports teams. Bob, his partners, and other business leaders won't claim full responsibility for the change, but they did help.

A LEGACY OF GIVING BACK

But the more important story about Bob and his partners is their legacy of giving back. He is an active member of Rotary, where he has given a lot of his time and money to support its causes. Another more impressive legacy is what his company has done over the years: built a culture of supporting various causes such as Lymphoma-Leukemia Society, ALS, and so many more. It all started with a meeting of his team to discuss what causes the company should support. One of his employee's family members suffered from leukemia so they all decided to support that cause. Then at another monthly meeting, another employee had a family member diagnosed with ALS, and that cause was added. At another meeting, a team member admitted that she had been battered in a past relationship, so they took up that cause as well. Today they support many organizations. In 2019, they were involved with eleven local charity events. Just check out their Community Involvement page on their website: https://www.brookside-optometric.com/community

The result of all this is a team that loves to work together because they have common goals to help others in the community. The morale at Brookside is very high and the team is excited to give more ideas. They enjoy their jobs so much they are naturally great promoters of the doctors and their work environment, as well.

Bob's company is not alone in building a culture of giving back. If you look up almost any of the Fortune 500, you will find they have a history of giving back in at least one way or another. In fact, many companies use their philanthropic efforts to recruit like-minded employees.

HELP OTHERS TO HELP YOURSELF

What is the bottom line here? When we work to help others, we feel better about ourselves, others, and our community!

What are you doing with your time and money to help your community?

Your answer might be something like, "I don't have anything to give!" or, "I don't have any time or money!" If you have been following this book and have completed most of the assignments, the second excuse should not be a valid one. And the first excuse is invalid, because we can all give something. It may be just helping to gather coats for the homeless in winter or as little as sharing that need and telling others how to donate through your social and business networks. Make some donation to your favorite charity and share that. Many people are asking for donations to a cause in lieu of gifts for a birthday/Christmas/anniversary/etc. Just start small. Once you start, you will want to do more and will work to find more ways to do so.

WHERE TO START

Not sure which you will start with? One way is to look to your family or friends to see if there is a cause that could help them. My mother-in-law died of Alzheimer's after many years of battling against it. I give regularly to find a cure. Bob's employees had friends and family that were suffering with various health issues that led them to support many causes. Ask your friends and peers what causes they are supporting for ideas. I am sure they would be very happy to invite you to join them. Another place to look is the various service clubs in your area like Rotary, Lions, and more.

Your assignment this week:

- Research a cause/nonprofit/community program you would like to promote.
- Seek out your employees for suggestions and to volunteer.
- Check with any of the current organizations you are already a member of for (additional) ways to get involved with their philanthropic activities.
- Review your activities on an annual basis. Life changes and so might your focus.

By getting involved with a great cause, your world will grow much larger, as will your self-esteem.

See you next week when we tackle regular expenses.

CHAPTER 35

WEEK 34—REVIEW FIXED EXPENSES AND PLAN FOR THE UNEXPECTED

"Be frugal, but not too frugal"

—DAVID, REGIONAL MANAGER, FOOD SERVICE OPERATIONS

David has been a successful regional manager for a couple of major food service chains over the many years that I have known him. But his previous employer really challenged his ongoing successes in the sector. David has years of experience from running his own restaurants as well as the chains he has worked for. He knows how to manage every aspect of the business, from food (quantity and quality) to employees, to marketing, and building management. He takes pride in his knowledge and skills to deliver great results.

TAKE CARE OF YOUR FACILITIES

David considered his employer to be too frugal and that frugality was the real challenge. Over the few years of working for them, he found it more and more difficult to retain customers even though he did a good job of managing all the budgets, food, and service quality. The main reason: The facilities were getting tired and shabby looking. Eventually they needed a total remodel which cost a lot more money than if the facilities were properly maintained and refreshed on a regular basis. He had to spend additional marketing money to woo the lost customers back and to attract new ones. All this because the company did not want to spend any money on maintenance when it was needed.

BEING PREPARED

Are you fully aware of your current expenses and potential unexpected ones? For example, one of my clients recently had to spend almost $900 for an unexpected repair on a large piece of equipment. Things are going to wear out and need maintenance or replacement. The safety of your staff and clientele is another consideration in maintaining your facilities. You may need to move to another location. Costs are ever increasing. And do you have the funds available when the unexpected occurs? See Week 39 for more information about this. Being fully aware of all these things will help you in making your annual budget, setting your prices, and preparing for future needs.

The theme for this week is to review your regular fixed expenses such as:

- Lease/rent—potential increases in price coming, time to renew, renegotiate, buyout, etc.
- Utilities—how to reduce use or increase efficiencies.
- Every day maintenance—cleaning, painting, etc.
- Long term maintenance—building, fixtures, equipment, etc.
- Replacement savings/budget—building, equipment, etc.
- What new regulations will require new/ongoing expenses (training, safety equipment, etc.)?
- Other agreements—Banking, credit, etc. Covered in Week 39
- Insurance—covered in Week 38

Your assignment this week:

- List all the regular expenses from your P & L and review— what can be modified or will change?

- List of all the items that will need maintenance this year and estimate costs.
- Make a schedule of what will need replacing and when—covering the next ten years.
- List of action items (lease agreements, etc.) that will need to be addressed this year and get them on your calendar.
- Review this exercise on an annual basis.

Planning and budgeting will save you a lot more now and down the road.

See you next week when we talk about vendors.

CHAPTER 36

WEEK 35—VENDOR REVIEW

"A smart manager will establish a culture of gratitude. Expand the appreciative attitude to suppliers, vendors, delivery people, and of course, customers."

—HARVEY MACKAY

Several new distributors had opened in my area. They were offering some great discounts along with promises of good service and fast deliveries. I had been making most of my purchases from a nearby supplier, but the lure of these new arrivals got the best of me, so I started shifting a few of my purchases to them. Some did have very low prices, but I soon discovered that the delivery time was slower than expected, the quality was dubious, and the warranty handling was often poor. This led to lost productivity in the shop and some not-so-happy customers when their repairs were delayed, or they had to return to the shop for unexpected repairs due to faulty parts. Another aspect of using lower priced items was a reduction in my profit margins (see Week 13 - Margins). The customer would get a lower price but at the cost of all my time, effort, and a lower profit margin.

Needless to say, my main supplier was not happy with the decrease in sales and stated so. He always gave me great service and, from time to time, extended the warranty of some components that failed just out of warranty. This made me and, more importantly, my customers happy. The more business I gave him, the more service I got from him. In the end I moved the majority of my business back to him.

IT GOES BOTH WAYS

This chapter has its weekly assignment for you to work on but comes with some sage wisdom that I, and many of my clients and fellow business owners, have learned over the years in working with many vendors. Working with vendors goes both ways: You treat them right and they do the same for you. As buyers, we are their customers. Every business has some customers that can be too 'high maintenance' and are not worth the time (see Week 48 - Fire Your Customer). You don't want to be one of those to your vendors.

When I first took over the operations of my service station, I continued to work with the vendors used by the previous owner. These vendors were already familiar with the location and the product inventory. As I started to inventory the stock (see Week 40 - Inventory) and deal with these vendors, it became clear who I needed to do more business with and who I needed to cease dealing with. I found it necessary to review them on a regular basis to give and get feedback on how each of us could do better for each other. This led to much better service, delivery, and pricing by being one of their best customers. Another perk was reduced dead stock on hand and an enhanced working relationship.

RESPECT YOUR VENDORS

I have worked on both sides of business as an owner and as a vendor. I find it shameful how some business owners treat their vendors. Whether you are buying inventory or services, some vendors do need to be fired. But most are just like you: they are business-people working hard to get and keep your business. And, like you, they are trying to make a living to take care of their families and personal needs. So, give them the respect they deserve.

Additional pieces of advice:

- Don't price shop your vendors and suppliers, whether it is someone who supplies what you may resell or what you need to run your business. This includes those that offer the various services you need. Consider all the services they offer, the value, quality, and time it costs you to work with them, and how it will affect the overall operation of your business and your bottom line. If you only look at price, you will have the same challenge with the clientele you deal with: We attract what we seek.

- Don't bully your vendors. The business owner that asks for spiffs every time the vendor shows up like tickets to shows or events, deeper discounts, bundle packages, promotional items are a challenge to vendors. Many hear comments like "I'm your best customer!" or, "I am making you rich!" or some other similar statements. How do you feel when any of your clients does the same to you? (And it is usually not your best customers!)

What if you treated your vendors as you would your employees or customers? What if you looked at them as part of what makes your business work and succeed? The better you treat them, the more they will do for you. We all work harder for those who appreciate us. And if one of your vendors is not responding in kind, find another. There are many others out there waiting to get your business.

Your assignment this week:

- Make a list of all your vendors (if you have not already done so).
- Set up a time to meet with them (if you have not already done so in another chapter) to review how things are going on both sides.
- If you have any inventory in stock (either for resale or supplies), ask for a review and adjustment at least annually.
- If the vendor has done a great job for you, take them to lunch or dinner or gift them something substantial.

When you complete this exercise, you will be amazed at the change in attitude of your vendors and how it will help your business.

See you next week where we look for an outsider's viewpoint

CHAPTER 37

WEEK 36— REVIEW BUSINESS WORKFLOW: GET SOME OUTSIDE HELP

———

"He was so lost he could not see the forest for the trees!"

— ANONYMOUS

Maylan Newton, owner of Educational Seminars Institute, offers a service where he will spend up to a week in a business watching and observing all that goes on in the business that hires him. He will spend the first two to three days just studying and taking notes. He listens to the conversations between the customers and employees, the employee to employee conversations, and the discourse between the owner and everyone else. He takes note of how inventory comes into the business, how the deliveries are handled, and how those items are sold to the clientele, tracked and billed. He watches how every aspect of the business proceeds. He has done this repeatedly in many businesses across the country.

By the third day, he has amassed enough information to give a thorough report to his client. He will review all this with the owner and give suggestions on how things as simple as a phone call can be improved. This process offers a unique viewpoint from an outside party that the business owner and many of the employees don't have. This will lead to some phenomenal improvements in the processes of the business.

Newton shared the story of one business owner who was complaining about the poor conversion rate he was getting on new customer calls becoming appointments. (A key KPI in Week 4). Since all the calls were being recorded, Maylan was able to listen in on the calls, check the number of unanswered calls, and compare them all to the number of appointments made to reveal the client's conversion rate. And yes, it was too low. Maylan also took the time to be in the business to watch and listen to the handling of the calls live. He was then able to coach his client and the staff on how to better handle the calls. The client just could not "see" the problem for himself.

The quote at the start of this chapter is like most of us as we go about our business. We all get caught up in our daily routines. But how many dollars are you losing to poor procedures? The last time you took a step back to look at your business (the forest) and the daily procedures (the trees) was in Week 9. But this step was an internal view taken by you and your team. This week's exercise is giving you an external view point. When have you ever sought the feedback from someone other than your employees? Here is a list of those you should consider asking for that outside, unbiased view of your business:

- Your best clients
- Your spouse
- Your best friend
- A business peer you respect
- An outside consultant—an industry expert or someone who does time and motion studies of businesses.

Once you perform this exercise you will be very much more enlightened, and surprised about the many aspects of how the work flows, or doesn't flow through your business.

Your assignment for this week:

- Bring in an outside individual or team to observe your business and give you feedback. This could be for just a few hours or a few days.
- Poll your customers, spouse, family, etc. for feedback. Your customer reviews process should be giving good feedback all the time.
- Sit down with your team and seek their feedback (you should be doing this in your team meetings already).
- Perform this on an annual basis.

See you next week where we apply the results of this activity to your business.

CHAPTER 38

WEEK 37—BUSINESS WORKFLOW: PROCEDURES— IMPLEMENTATION

───

"Successful organizations understand the importance of implementation, not just strategy, and, moreover, recognize the crucial role of their people in this process."

—JEFFREY PFEFFER

How many workshops or seminars have you attended where you get a ton of great ideas? You take some notes, highlight some of the lines in the workbook and maybe dogear a few of the pages. You do all this so when you get back to work you can implement all those wonderful ideas! And what happens? Most of us get overwhelmed with the list because we never take the time to prioritize the ideas and the urgent call of business distracts us from implementing few, if any, of them.

What I learned in doing my many workshops over the years is to help my attendees by giving each of them a special sheet titled The Green Sheet. They are to put all their ideas on the sheet as they get them and place a dollar amount for what that idea might be worth if implemented in the business. The dollar valuation is a great motivator. At the end of the workshop I ask that they review the list and pick the top three to implement when they get back to work. The rest can be done at another time (if ever!). I find this to be very effective and less overwhelming.

Your assignment this week is the follow-up to last week's exercise of observing the procedures in your business. In reviewing the list generated by the exercise, keep the following in mind:

- How can the procedure(s) be improved?
- Who should be involved in this? Employee(s), your spouse, your coach/mentor, a fellow business owner?
- What costs might be incurred? (Equipment, furniture, electronics, fixtures, etc.)

- How much time will be needed to implement this? (Training, logistics, etc.)
- How much time will it take for everyone to accept and adapt?

The goal is to find the best way to get the change(s) implemented without overwhelming you or your team. Depending on the new/revised procedure, new habits take time to build, but keep at it. Understand that it will take more time than a week for most changes to take hold. Keep an open mind as you will probably need to make some modifications as you go.

Your assignment this week:

- Take the list of issues presented and put a dollar amount on each (what they are worth to the business in either increased productivity and/or sales, how much savings to the business or better employee morale).
- Choose the top three.
- Apply the questions mentioned above to your three choices on how best to address the issues.
- Keep this list of all the issues handy as you apply the suggestions and address them going forward.
- This exercise should be annualized like many others.

See you next week for the next 1 Thing!

CHAPTER 39

WEEK 38—REVIEW YOUR INSURANCE POLICIES

"There are worse things in life than death. Have you ever spent an evening with an insurance salesman?"

—WOODY ALLEN

Alvaro was a software client of mine for several years. When I decided to try my hand at insurance through the advice of a friend (yes, I have done several different things in my life, but all have prepared me for writing this book!) I approached him to see if I could help him with his insurance. I reviewed his current policies and discovered that not only was he under-insured, but missing some very important coverage, as well. I was able to give him better coverage and at a better rate. He had been with the same agent for many years and had never asked for a policy review nor sought out other potential vendors. Had I not approached him and if he had to file a claim, he could have been in some serious financial trouble, if not out of business altogether!

IT'S A PART OF DOING BUSINESS

No one likes to talk insurance, shop it, and much less having to buy it. But it is a fact of life that we must have it to protect us from the unexpected for our business and employees.

Things change in our business and life often. We all need good advisors to meet with on a regular basis at different intervals. You contact your agent whenever you have an immediate change, but you should sit down and discuss your policies and coverage on an annual basis. It is usually best to do so when you get your renewal notice about 90 days out from expiration.

Some things to consider:

- What has changed in your business: status change in the business such as incorporating, a new partner, additions to the facility, new equipment, expansion or contraction.
- Appetites (what risks an insurance company likes to cover) change and how that may mean a significant

change in your rates—up or down. Ask your broker about this.

- Are you sure about your coverage and what it all means? If not, take the time to ask.
- New laws like employment regulations, hazardous waste/ materials, ADA, and more may mean new types of coverage that you don't currently have. Two areas that were unheard of several years ago are Employment Liability and Data Breach coverage.
- Are you looking to offer any/more employee benefits?
- Life insurance—for you, a key employee, a partner and/ or group coverage.
- If you are leasing your property, are there any changes in the lease that requires more or different insurance coverage?
- Does your personal coverage on your home and auto have enough liability coverage? Ask about umbrella coverage for both your personal and business assets.
- Do you ever do some outside event (presentations, parties, etc.)? If not covered by the venue you rent, you may need some event coverage.
- Is your agent/broker proactively in contact with you about your policies and more?

Your assignment this week:

- Set up a time to meet with your agent/broker to discuss/ review your policies.
- Seek out another agent/broker or two for a quote and opinion on coverage.
- Ask your peers what coverage they have and from whom.
- Look to your business association for advice.

You might find out that your long-term relationship has not been so good or that it just needs a jolt to get them on track. Anyone can fall into the trap of complacency.

Next up we talk more money—banking and more.

CHAPTER 40

WEEK 39—REVIEW YOUR BANKING, CREDIT CARDS, ETC.

"Banks do not create money for the public good. They are businesses owned by private shareholders. Their purpose is to make a profit."

— JOHN ROGERS, *LOCAL MONEY: WHAT DIFFERENCE DOES IT MAKE?*

Rob was enticed by his banker to have the bank take over the handling of his credit card processing. After all, weren't they the folks who already handled all his banking needs? It would only make sense to have them handle his credit card processing as well, especially with the enticing promise of having the funds deposited in his bank account the very next day, along with a competitive interchange rate (the percentage charged on each transaction). All this would be handled with only a two-year agreement.

THE FINE PRINT

Like most of us, Rob was a trusting soul and expected the bank had his best interest in mind. But he did not read the small print on the agreement before signing it. In that agreement was a mention of the ability of the bank to raise the rates as they chose during that two-year agreement. And, like many other busy business owners, Rod did not notice the increases until many months later. The increases weren't outrageous, but still nothing to be happy about nor could he do anything about it. As time went by, he neglected to check on these fees after the expiration of the agreement because it was his bank, and they were taking care of him and it would be too much trouble to go to another processor.

This story is not just Rob's. I have seen many others (me included, I hate to admit) that have been in the same situation.

The focus of this week's agenda is for you to review your bank, credit card processing, equipment leases, loans, and any other institution that you deal with when it comes to handling your money.

CHECK THE EXPIRATION DATE

Do you have any leases about to expire? Some leases come with some very poor terms such as a large buyout or an auto-renewal clause that requires at thirty-day or more notice to terminate or exercise a buyout prior to the expiration date. Going forward, be very aware of what happens at the end of any lease you agree to. I suggest to all my clients and friends to seek a $1 buyout option at the end of the lease. Yes, you will pay a bit more per month, but you will have the option to buy out cheaply at the end or opt to return the equipment and then buy or lease a newer model.

What other financial obligations do you have? Do you know all the rates, fees, conditions (early payoff terms, buyouts, rate changes, etc.) that can affect your cash flow? You should be reviewing your obligations at least annually and to schedule any due dates or key change dates on your calendar. Loan payments don't show on your profit and loss statements (the interest does) but will appear on your cash flow reports. You need to make sure these payments are in your budget when planning your year.

When it comes to merchant services (credit card processing), be wary of those that guarantee the lowest prices on the processing fees or a long-term agreement to lock in prices or equipment packages. Look for those that offer excellent service, free or low-cost equipment with a fast turnaround time for replacement equipment, and no contracts. I have seen too many businesses sign up for a five-year agreement and are still using old equipment that is no longer secure to use. Why? Because their processor wanted them to sign up for a new agreement just to get new equipment.

Are you paying high interest rates on loans or have high lease payments on equipment? Maybe it's time to refinance some of the agreements. Or maybe sell off that piece of equipment you hardly use, or possibly outsource that service to another company. One example is printers. There are many options to choose from: leasing, purchasing, support programs, pay-by-the-page printed or using a printing company.

Whenever you are seeking better terms, look at the small print and don't just look at the lowest rate. Sometimes an enticing low rate is just a teaser to get your business and you end up paying a much higher rate after an introductory period and/or there is a very high penalty for early payoff.

What fees are you paying for your bank to handle your checking and other transactions? Are you getting the best rate on any savings you have there? Are the services offered competitive? Just like reviewing your vendors (Week 35) on a regular basis, your banker should be among this group, as well. If you haven't shopped for banking in a while, now is the time to do so. You may be quite surprised by what you find—good or bad.

PLAN AHEAD FOR YOUR FINANCING NEEDS

I received the following business lending advice from my longtime friend Joe Monte of TB Business Finance.

"There are several business lending companies that take advantage of the fact that a bank loan takes sixty days or more to obtain. These non-bank lenders are quick, but I have seen rates as high as 35 percent. An excellent way to avoid this cost is to apply for a business line of credit now. You will have cash available when you need it. Next, for known upcoming needs, apply for a loan at least ninety days before you need the money.

To qualify for a bank loan, you need enough NOI (Net Operating Income) to support the payments. Review your bookkeeping. Capital improvements and equipment should be on the balance sheet as an asset that you depreciate over several years. If you write that new roof off as repairs and maintenance, it will lower your NOI and not show an increase of business worth on your balance sheet. These add up. Even a new printer can be capitalized. I know one client who has done a lot of improvements and construction over the years and he now writes off $600,000 per year in depreciation. He can make $600,000 profit before he has any tax liability."

Your assignment this week is:

- Make a list of all the agreements you have (leases, loans, lines of credit, services, maintenance contracts, etc.)
- Review the expiration dates and any requirements attached to those dates (auto renewals, rate increases, buy-outs, etc.)
- Place those pertinent dates on your calendar as future action items. Any that need immediate attention, address them this week.
- Make notes on this list of any that can be renegotiated now or be shopped for better rates or services.
- Start your search for bankers and leasing/loan agents. Your network is a good place to start. (See Week 46 - Networking)

If you perform this task on an annual basis you will have fewer issues with your cash flow and have a greater sense of control of your business.

Next up: we talk stock!

CHAPTER 41

WEEK 40—INVENTORY: TRACK AND MANAGE IT

———

"The more inventory a company has, the less likely they will have what they need."

— JTAIICHI OHNOAL'S

Al's Seafood Restaurant in Baltimore was the featured restaurant in a June 2017 episode of Restaurant Impossible on the Food Network. One of many of the issues addressed was their inventory control of the food—it was non-existent. They had too much food in stock, had no idea of the content thereof, and most of it was rotten because no one knew how long it had been there. Sadly, they had to throw away thousands of dollars' worth of food. The solution was to set up processes and procedures for how the food would be ordered, used while still fresh, and who would be responsible for the inventory.

LEARNED MY OWN LESSON

The inventory was included as part of the purchase price of my business. I went to work getting to know my vendors, how they worked, handled my stock, and their warranties and exchange policies. I was about to return all the stock from one vendor because of their less-than-stellar reputation when it came to quality, but the vendor was adamant about his product being so good that he offered to pay any warranty labor for replacement of any failed product. Less than six months later, I had a problem with the parts we installed on a customer's vehicle. It took about an hour or two for us to confirm the customer's complaint and to verify the new parts' failure. We replaced defective parts with a known good manufacturer which performed much better. The next time the vendor came in to restock, I presented him with the bad parts and submitted a request for the warranty labor I had to pay my technician. He responded with, "I can only credit your labor request toward any purchases you make today and will give you free replacement of the defective parts." This was not acceptable to me. So, I took the loss and dismissed the vendor. I realized I had made the mistake of not going with my initial feelings about the (bad) product and for not reading the entire product warranty policy.

To make this story even more frustrating, when the new vendor was removing all the old parts and swapping in the new lines, I was informed that I had far more stock than necessary. Much of the stock was so obsolete I probably would never had sold it all! From then on, I took much more interest in my inventories, including my business operations supplies.

There are several lessons here:

- Have an inventory control/tracking program.
- Always be aware of warranty and return policies with your vendors/manufacturers.
- Use vendors that offer to trade out slower moving items.
- Stock only what you really need to keep business flowing. You don't want staff idle while waiting for a product delivery or turning customers away.
- Know what you have on the shelves. Is it current, fashionable, and applicable to you what you service, and what is useful in the processes of your business?
- Establish the person(s) responsible for managing your inventory.
- Know your turn-rate—how often you turn over the items in inventory. You should be able to do this through your product sales reports.

- Ask your vendor for a volume discount on fast-moving items, if you have not already done so.
- Ask your vendor for consignment of stocking items. This can save you cash flow and your vendor should help you manage the inventory better—they want to move more stock, as well.
- Don't stock any items you can get delivered to you in the time you need it, unless it is a very fast-moving item and can get a volume discount.
- Supplies inventory should be monitored as well, to avoid waste, overstock, and pilferage.
- Set up a purchase ordering system so that you can track where the purchases are applied.
- Talk to your accountant about the method you should be using to account for the value of your inventory.

Your assignment this week:

- Review the list above
- Figure out what your most pressing need(s) is/are.
- Review or set up system(s) for managing your inventory and to address the issues that may affect your business.

Once you get your systems in place, review this on an annual basis, if not more often. It will save you a lot of money and time.

Next week is about association!

CHAPTER 42

WEEK 41—JOIN YOUR BUSINESS ASSOCIATION

"A man only learns in two ways, one by reading, and the other by association with smarter people."

—WILL ROGERS

Paul Grech was a typical new business owner: He didn't know what he didn't know when he got started. He ran a good business and was doing OK. One day he learned about the statewide business organization for his industry and the potential benefits he might enjoy by joining. He signed up and started attending the local chapter meetings where he gained a lot more knowledge about what the association had to offer. He also learned a lot from fellow members through the networking at the meetings. He started attending some of the workshops hosted by the association. Then at one of the chapter meetings, the guest speaker said something that changed his life: buy your building and take control of your future. Paul credits this one thing as the choice that really turned his life and business around. Today, Paul is retired but still attends the chapter meetings with regularity. He is a big proponent of being part of the association and continues to be an ambassador for it. He still owns the building he bought and is leasing it out to another business owner that now helps to fund his retirement.

MORE THAN JUST EDUCATION

As long as I have been a business owner, in whatever field I have been in, I sought out and joined that industry's association. Like Paul, the main reasons I joined were to network, learn from the other members, to take advantage of the educational programs, and to support the lobbying efforts of the association. Many members, like myself, find the meetings very beneficial in discussing operational issues and so much more. If challenged by an operational issue, you can reach out to a fellow member for advice. You will discover you can learn so much more than just attending a webinar or a workshop. Some enjoy the meetings but find the other educational programs more suitable to their learning styles when looking to expand their business knowledge.

The other benefits of an association usually include discounts on services, products and equipment relative to the industry. In some cases, you can get services through the group that you cannot get on your own.

YOUR ADVOCATE

As I mentioned above, most groups have a lobbying aspect to them—their advocate, their voice in government. These groups work to inform local, state, and, in some cases, national legislators on how pending or needed legislation can dramatically affect the industry and many times its clients. I have attended several "Legislative Days" where the industry group individuals meet with legislators to discuss legislation and other industry issues affected by governmental regulation. These events have been eye opening for me as well as the legislators. The larger your group membership is, the more they have a voice in the halls of government. You owe it to your industry to become a member.

THE NEXT LEVEL

By now you have probably figured out that I am a joiner. I admit it. I will tell you something else about me: I often take my membership to the next level by taking on a leadership role. You should do the same once you have settled into membership. You will get more out of your membership by getting on the board, joining a committee, or volunteering to help in any capacity. You will grow in many ways when you do, and it will enhance your business indirectly.

Another organization you should consider joining is your local Chamber of Commerce (mentioned in Week 46 - Networking). Chambers offer a lot of the same as the industry associations, but on a local level. Leveraging time is key to success in life and business, so let organizations like the Chamber do some of the work you may not have time to do. Chambers have many events like networking events (known as mixers), business education classes, social and civic events, and other forums that differ from your associations.

Your assignment for this week:

- Seek out and join your industry's association.
- If you are already a member, time to get on a committee, the Board, or take on some event planning.
- Attend an extracurricular event like Legislative Day. If you have not done this before, maybe it's time to do so this year.
- Attend some of the local Chamber events.

Don't over obligate yourself, but the more involved you are, the more you will get out of membership in any organization.

Next week is all about getting a good education! But that is what this whole book is about.

CHAPTER 43

WEEK 42—GOOD EDUCATION IS CHEAP. THE RIGHT EDUCATION IS PRICELESS.

———

"Learning is not attained by chance, it must be sought for with ardor and diligence"

—ABIGAIL ADAMS

The high school I attended was, and still is, considered to be one of the best in the state. My daughter, who now lives in that area, tells me that her local friends are impressed when she mentions I went there. And, yes, I received a great education there. I got some good education from the local junior college, especially in my field of endeavor. The college even provided me with a good Introduction to Business class. All good things to know but what they, and all other schools, did not give me, was the right education on being a small business owner. When I finally got my own business, there was a lot I didn't know about what I didn't know—just like many other business owners.

THE ANSWER IS NOT MORE HOURS

I often tell others that I was successful in business mainly because I made up for my lack of business knowledge by working more hours. In a typical week I worked six days and anywhere from ten to fifteen hours each day! On-the-job training seems to be the mantra for many business owners, and I was no exception. I learned how to work with customers and keep them happy (my employees said I had a silver tongue), do some decent marketing, keep a team of employees working long hard hours, and make a decent living while doing so. A lot of trial and error was part of the package! I learned much from those I worked for and with over the years, but still had issues that could have been avoided had I received some formal business education. Like many businesses, my cash flow was inconsistent even though I was doing a lot of business. My accountant would give me some good advice from time to time, but that was still not enough.

THE RIGHT EDUCATION

How was I to get out of the ups and downs of business and stop working so many hours? I needed to get the right education. But where? The formal education system does not teach any small business classes. I just happened to hear about some business operations classes run by a successful shop owner. He gave me information that helped me to set up some pricing systems, productivity-tracking tools, and more things that would increase my profits immensely. This was the start of my ongoing search of more business knowledge. I wish I had taken more classes earlier in my career—a lament that many others before me and after me have made. The end result of getting the right education was a very profitable business that I was able to sell for a very nice sum several years later.

The typical business owner tends to go to classes on how to do what they do in their business: a baker learns more about baking, the doctor about medicine, and so on. Yes, knowing the most you can about your craft is important, but the best in any field can fail if the business side is not properly set up and run profitably. What every business owner needs is good business education on how to work on the business.

Look for classes on business education that cover:

- people skills
- budgets
- pricing
- marketing
- HR issues
- sales (even doctors need this!)
- managing teams
- KPIs (Week 4 - Knowing Your Numbers)
- planning

What areas do you struggle with in your business? There are classes, workshops, seminars, webinars, coaches, online self-study, industry conferences, and books (I have a suggested reading list on my site and in the appendix?) that are available to educate you. Seek out your peers, your industry associations, places like SCORE, a good business coach, and trade or business journals for the availability of opportunities to learn.

Your assignment this week:

- Sign up for at least one business class/workshop every year that covers your weakest or most challenging area.
- Attend industry events that have training classes and/or presenting speakers.

- Start reading. Find a business/management/team/marketing book to read or listen to. Make it a goal to read at least four books this year. Another great saying: "Readers are leaders."

Get the right education and you will be much better off at the end of this year and every year thereafter. Your future self will thank you.

Up next week is educating yourself about your customers.

CHAPTER 44

WEEK 43—KNOW YOUR CUSTOMERS AND FOLLOW UP.

"The more you engage with customers the clearer things become and the easier it is to determine what you should be doing."

—JOHN RUSSELL

DO YOU KNOW YOUR BEST CLIENTS?

At the time of writing this, we have lived in the same house for over thirty-five years. In that time, we have visited a local sewing machine and vacuum cleaner sales and repair store many, many times. My wife has bought sewing machine pieces and parts and had our vacuum and steam cleaners repaired there multiple times. The last time I was in there, I was replacing a vacuum cleaner that had broken a second time and decided to buy a top-of-the-line industrial brand unit instead. The owner suggested that the brand I was buying was much more reliable—which it has been. But in all this time, none of the people that work there (I presume it is the owners since the faces have not changed) know our names nor have they recognized us anytime we visit. They have never asked for any information from us. They still write up every sale on an old-fashioned carbonless receipt book! Maybe they don't feel it is important since they have a unique business, but one must presume they are slowly losing business to the internet and more.

WHY GET A PROGRAM

What is one important thing this shop should do? Get a *"Point of Sale"* (POS) program that can gather their customers' information (and help with the bookkeeping!). As mentioned in other chapters, seek for an industry specific program, but if nothing else, get Quickbooks or Peachtree like system. Then, add a *"Customer Relationship Management"* (CRM) program (if not part of the POS). Why? To automate the follow up on your clientele. There are many reasons, and here are just a few:

- To keep in touch with the customer. The competition is marketing to them, so why not you? It is far less expensive to keep a customer than to get a new one. Touch marketing is very key to keeping your clientele.
- Get to know the value of the customer. How much do they spend with you? What is it they buy? What do they own/eat/need that you can offer more for them to come back and more often?
- Get more referrals. Offer referral bonuses. Send them vital information related to the services you offer, not just for them to buy more, but value-added stories and articles.
- Follow-up on recent purchases with thank you notes and surveys on the product and/or service
- Sends reminders of future appointments, needed services, feature updates, added/new services offered, etc.
- Give you many of the KPIs and reports spoken of in Week 4.

Your assignment this week:

- Follow up system—set one up or is it time for an upgrade? Make sure it can be automated to save you time to run the business.
- Point of sale program—set one up or is it time for an upgrade?

- Review the statistics of your current program(s) and set up a time in your calendar to get these on a regular basis.

Go to www.1week1thing.com to view the *"Lifetime Value of a Customer"* sheet.

You should review the numbers of this program regularly just as you would your monthly bookkeeping reports but do a full review on an annual basis. This will help you with your marketing and budget plans.

See you next week when we talk about time.

CHAPTER 45

WEEK 44—REVIEW HOURS OF OPERATION AND STAFFING

———

"What's the one constant in the universe? Change."

—JEFFREY NOTT

Original Joe's Italian restaurant has been a business in downtown San Jose since 1956. They have been a staple in the area serving lunches and dinners and a meeting place for many local organizations. They have had their challenges with the ups and downs of the economy over the years and adjusted to survive. But they had to make a major change recently. For years, they entertained the many local business folk for

lunch, but with the advent of many local high-tech companies offering free food in their own kitchens and the changing dining choices of the younger workers, their lunchtime
crowds disappeared. Because of this, they closed their doors
for lunch on weekdays.[28]

What if this happened in your business? How would you
handle this issue if you had to reduce staff?

DO YOU REALLY NEED ALL THOSE PEOPLE?

I heard the story of a similar issue at a restaurant that needed
to cut staff due to slow business but didn't want to lay off
anyone or cut hours. The staff was a good team and, as every
employer knows, it is hard to find and keep good people. The
owner decided to bring the issue up at a team meeting. He
stated the problem and asked for suggestions. As it turned
out, one employee wanted a couple of days off to stay with
her children, another wanted less hours so they could attend
more school, and others wanted to work different shifts. The
reason they did not bring up their desires beforehand was
because of fear that they might not get the hours they wanted
or be fired. The result was the business saved not only the
money on wages but saved the team, as well.

---

28 Sal Pizarro, Original Joe's Closing for Lunch? Say it ain't so! (San
Jose Mercury News) https://bayareane.ws/2BlI30L (February 1, 2019)

Questions to consider on an annual basis or as the market changes:

- Are you open during the hours you need to be open to properly service your clientele? Are you opening/closing too soon or too late? The right days?
- When is/are your busiest time(s)/day(s)?
- Do you have the right people covering at the right hours?
- Do you have too many or too few on staff?
- Do you talk about the business flow in your team meetings? Do you ask the team for feedback?
- What are the competitors doing in your area hours wise? What do you need to do to stay competitive?

Your assignment this week:

- Review your business hours and staffing.
- Meet with your team as needed.
- Adjust to meet the needs of your business but more importantly, your clientele.

Be open to making changes and don't get stuck on, *"We've always done it this way."* It could cost you employees and clientele.

Next week is all about delegation and staying alive.

CHAPTER 46

WEEK 45—DELEGATE OR DIE

———

"There's a big difference between being self-employed and being a business owner. Being self-employed feels like freedom until you realize that if you take time off, your business crumbles. To be a true business owner, make it so that you could leave for a year, and when you came back, your business would be doing better than when you left."

—DEREK SIVERS—*ANYTHING YOU WANT - 40 LESSONS FOR A NEW KIND OF ENTREPRENEUR*

CD-Baby had grown from one employee with total sales of over $1,000,000 in 1999 to eighty-five employees closing in on $4,000,000 sales per month in 2007. Business was growing faster than he ever expected. He started the business just to help independent musicians get their music sold. But with eighty-five employees, he was being sought out by them many times a day just to ask him simple questions. *"The customer ordered two CDs but did so on two different orders and wants to know if they can be shipped together to save on shipping. What should I do?" "Some guy wants to know if he can pay by wire transfer." "A guy wants to know if we can change his album art even though we already posted it."* This went on from 7 a.m. to 10 p.m. every day! One day Derek snapped and just left and stayed home for a few days, but finally realized he needed to fix the problem and not hide from it. He had to make himself unnecessary to the business.

He went back to work, but when someone came to him with a question, he called the team together to discuss how it should be handled. They came up with solutions and a policy, put it in the policy manual, and went back to his office. He did this for every question that came up over the next two months until there were no more questions. Everyone was empowered to handle the issues and if they did not know how, they referred to the policy manual. Derek was now free to do other things only he could do in the business and the day-to-day went on without him.[29]

---

29 Derek Sivers, *Anything You Want - 40 Lessons for a New Kind of Entrepreneur* (Brilliance Audio, 2011)

CAN YOU WALK AWAY?

Can you be like Derek and walk away from your business for a day, a week, or a month, and have the business still run the same? If not, why not? Many of the previous chapters have addressed making the many processes and procedures of your business run better. But what are you still doing that may be keeping you tied down and having to be in the business every day? Maybe it's time to start trusting your team and do some delegating. And the delegating of what you do is not limited to your employees. There are other things that you probably should outsourcing.

So just what are the things that you are doing every day? This would be the first step to discover what you might be able to delegate. What policies need to be in place, and how can you empower your team? You must be willing to let go and trust others to make some decisions. If you train them right, they can do what you do and set yourself free from being tied down to the business. If you ever want to expand your business in size and/or to multiple locations, this exercise is a must.

Your assignment this week:

- List all the things you do that someone else could do instead. This could be anything from handling the mundane issues like in Derek's business to posting things on your business social media sites.

- Make a policy and procedure to address each of the things that could be handled by your team instead of you.
- Hire others to do things like your social media postings, bookkeeping, etc.
- You may need to take a little more time in the next few weeks to work on this (like Derek) as you build the policies and procedures, but you will have more time once completed.

Delegating will not only give your more time to work on the business and have time away from the business, but it will enhance the value of your business if you ever decide to sell. A savvy potential business buyer won't want to buy a job but will want to buy a business that can run successfully without them.

See you next week where we expand your network.

CHAPTER 47

WEEK 46—BE A PEOPLE PERSON: GET OUT AND NETWORK

"Now, there's a reason mom said 'Be a people person!' and there are many reasons why it's good to be an extrovert (or act like one). One big reason is they make more money."

— ERIC BARKER, *BARKING UP THE WRONG TREE*

Alejandro has the opportunity to expand his business. The business next door to him in the same building had just moved out. His business coach asked me to join him in looking at the facility and to give Alejandro some advice. In the process of discussing all the various things he would have to do to make the space usable for his business, I suggested he contact the local Chamber of Commerce. I told him of my experience in working with my local Chamber and how it had been of immense help in working with other business owners looking to expand or just set up shop in my city. The Chamber helps many business owners when they must deal with permits and more. I have seen many a business avoid many delays just by employing the services and connections of the Chamber.

GO FORTH AND MAKE CONNECTIONS.

Connections—we all need them—in our business and personal lives. No one goes it alone. The more connections you have, the more successful you will be. Studies have proved this over and over. Even those beneath the law know the power of networking! Gang members, in and out of prison, rely on their own networks to protect themselves and to enhance their *"business."* The Mafia knows the power of connections! Eric Barker points this out in his book and recalls many stories of the success of those who are connected with other more successful individuals in their field[30]. I have networked for years, which has not only given me more business, but has given me many resources that I can use outside of business. Many of the stories and the information in this

---

30 Eric Barker, *Barking Up The Wrong Tree* (New York: Harper One)

book have come from the people I have met while networking. I frequently get requests from friends and business contacts asking me for referrals to help them with everything from car repair to phone systems.

EXTROVERT OR INTROVERT? BOTH WORK!

If you are an extrovert, you probably have a large network already. If you are an introvert, you will have to challenge yourself to get out and network. Many introverts do so successfully and so can you.

Where do you start networking? There are many places to start:

- A Leads/Referral group—there are many in every city, such as BNI (the biggest). These groups are made up of many of the local businesses (usually only one per industry in each club) where you meet others, present your business via a thirty-second commercial and exchange leads and referrals. The more tenured and formal members of these groups will help the first-timer learn how to make commercials and give/get leads. These can be a great source of business for you. Groups range in size and businesses, with some that are just for professionals like attorneys, bankers, CPAs, and the like. Feel free to check out several of them before committing to one.

- Chamber of Commerce—if you haven't yet joined your local Chamber, this is the week to do so. You might be in a location like me where there are several chambers in the area. You might join them all or just one. Typically, I encourage people to join the Chamber where their business is located but if they do all their business in another nearby city, join that one. Visit each and get to know a few members to get a good idea about which you should join. My local Chambers host annual HR, Labor Law and Tax updates seminars for free (in most cases) to members. If you are already a member, it's time to step up and get a bit more involved. You will be richly rewarded.

- Service Groups—Rotary, Masons, Religious organizations, Lions, etc. You join them to be part of what they do, not to get business directly. Once you get active in a group and they get to know you, the business will follow. Look for one that you feel matches your beliefs and/or interests.

- Toastmasters—if you want to learn to speak and/or present to people this is a great place to start and a great way to make new friends and naturally get some business.

- Look for other groups online like MeetUp for other places to network. It doesn't have to be all about business, but it will have an effect on you and your business. They have many different special interest groups and I am sure you will find one that interests you.

Your assignment this week:

- Schedule time this week, or in the following weeks, to visit some groups or add more to your existing groups.
- Visit one of the local Chambers mixers. You can attend as a guest to see if it is right for you.

Not a mixer? Many of these offer tips on how to best network. So, get out and meet some people before next week's assignment. You can talk about your use of this book as a topic as you mingle!

Up next week: more talk about money. Yay!

CHAPTER 48

WEEK 47—PAY YOURSELF FIRST.

———

"I found the road to wealth when I decided that a part of all I earned was mine to keep."

—ARKAD, *THE RICHEST MAN IN BABYLON*

Gary Meisner was a fellow Shell Dealer and a very successful one at that. He had done so well that he was able to buy the property and the building when the Oil company offered it up for sale. I did not know his real secret to success until several years later, when I was selling automotive software programs.

When we were discussing the purchase of my software programs, he told me that he would purchase them as soon as he could make sure it would not affect his paying himself first. I understood the concept but was stymied that he would not invest in my programs first, which would theoretically increase his profits thereby guaranteeing his payments to himself. He told me that he had a strict regimen and would not deviate from it as doing so for many years helped him to buy his property (in Palo Alto, Calif., a very pricey area even in 1996) and much more.

He eventually bought my software programs, but his story has stuck with me for many years. This concept was reinforced to me when I read *The Richest Man in Babylon*[31] a few years ago. A short summary of main points the book:

- Save a portion of all you earn
- Do not confuse your necessary expenses with your desires
- Work hard to improve your skills because wealth is the result of a reliable income stream
- Full success comes when you overcome the spirit of procrastination within yourself

---

31 George Classon, *The Richest Man in Babylon* (New York: Signet Publishing, 1988)

SELLING YOUR BUSINESS?

So many business owners never pay themselves very much nor do they put any money away even if they do pay themselves well. Many are hoping to sell their business for a tidy profit when they finally retire, but all too many find out too late that their business is either not sell-able, not worth what they thought it would be, or they lose their lease and find themselves out of business. If this might be you, get a true valuation of your business right away. Better to find out now than later. Seek out a business broker to get you a valuation. Remember a business is only worth what someone else will pay you for it. More on business valuation at www.1week1thing.com Once you get through this entire book and implement all that I have suggested, your business should have increased in value!

What can you do instead? There are many options. But the first step is just to start putting something away (10 percent is a popular amount) on a regular basis. Once you get in the habit, it gets easier to do. If you have reached this part of the book and have successfully completed the previous chapter's tasks, you should be making more money and can easily afford to save. The first thing you should save up for is a ninety-day (minimum) rainy day fund to cover all your living expenses in case the business is closed for a stint.

Where else to put your money? There are many areas:

- Stocks, bonds, mutual funds
- Real property—investment and/or your business building
- College savings—if you have any children or grandchildren
- Life insurance—there are some great savings plans built into some policies
- Other businesses—ever thought of expanding?
- Travel fund—it'd be nice to pay all cash for that next trip
- IRA/Roth/401K

Like everything else, you should have a plan and seek out some professional assistance. You should know what you have in mind for your future needs and the money it will take to meet those needs.

Your assignment this week:

- Start a simple savings plan—automate a percent or $ amount to be deposited in your rainy-day fund
- Seek out others you know that are successful in their investments
- Seek out a professional financial adviser to start a conversation
- Set a time to review your financial status on an annual basis to adjust as needed.

"To the building of an estate there must always be the beginning."—Arkad, *The Richest Man in Babylon*

See you next week, when we get to tackle the bad customer. (Not literally, but you might like to!)

CHAPTER 49

WEEK 48—FIRE YOUR CUSTOMER!

———

"The customer isn't always right!"

— QUOTED BY MANY AUTHORS!

The woman frequently flew on Southwest but was disappointed with every aspect of the company's operation. In fact, she became known as the *"Pen Pal"* because after every flight she wrote in with a complaint.

She didn't like the fact that the company didn't assign seats; she didn't like the absence of a first-class section; she didn't like not having a meal in flight; she didn't like Southwest's boarding procedure; she didn't like the flight attendants' sporty uniforms and the casual atmosphere. And she hated peanuts! Her last letter, reciting a litany of complaints, momentarily stumped Southwest's customer relations people.

Sherry Phelps, a Director of Corporate Employment at Southwest, explains: "Southwest prides itself on answering every letter that comes to the company and several employees tried to respond to this customer, patiently explaining why we do things the way we do them. [Our response] was quickly becoming a [large] volume until they bumped it up to Herb's desk, with a note: 'This one's yours.'

In sixty seconds, Kelleher wrote back and said, 'Dear Mrs. Crabapple, We will miss you. Love, Herb.'[32]"

VOTE 'EM OUT!

A friend of mine runs a payroll company. During his team's first meeting in each December, they discuss which client is the most troublesome to deal with. They discuss those clients that call every pay period with one challenge or another or demand last minute changes or extensions over the deadlines to submit their employees' hours and more. After some discussion, they vote who they will *"extend an invitation"*

---

32 Duran, How Southwest Lost a Customer (Blob: Medium.com)
    https://bit.ly/2EJHCZA (July 7, 2016)

to find another payroll company that the client might be happier with.

I once had a customer who came to my shop to just get an oil change service and never anything more. His car had many obvious problems, but he refused to have them repaired. Every time he came in, there were more problems that needed some serious attending to, but he only purchased the basic service. The last time he came in for a service, he mentioned that there was a new problem with the motor mounts. He did not want to fix them, he just wanted me to be aware of it. As I pulled the vehicle into the service bay, the motor almost jumped out of the engine compartment, locking the throttle to full acceleration. Due to my good training over the years, I quickly turned off the ignition before I drove the vehicle through the back wall of the shop. After we pushed the vehicle out of the shop and with my heart still pounding, I did everything in my power to politely tell the customer that we would never do any service work for him again.

IT'S JUST A MARKETING PHRASE

The phrase, *"The customer is always right,"* was originally coined in 1909 by Harry Gordon Selfridge, the founder of Selfridge's department store in London.[33] He made it up as

33 Kerjulf, Top 5 Reasons Why 'The Customer is Always Right' is Wrong. (Blog: Huffpost) https://bit.ly/2Y3Q1fy (April 15, 2015)

a marketing tool! Many businesses still use this phrase in training employees and working with their customers.

But anyone who has worked with customers on any level can share many stories that prove the customer is not always right. They can be mean, demanding, dishonest, slow to pay, don't follow directions and take up a lot of your time. There are those that buy almost nothing from you but expect to be treated like they are your best customer. They are morale killers for your team, especially if you persist with Harry Gordon's phrase. This can lead to higher turnover if employees must pander to every customer—right or wrong.

These bad players not only take up extra time to deal with, but they rob precious time away from good clients. And how does it look to your good client, or worse, a prospect, when they see you dealing with bad customers? Even when you are not at fault, this could cause you to lose the good ones. Impressions are powerful and hard to overcome once set in place.

NOT EVERYONE IS YOUR CUSTOMER

Ever have one of those customers that no matter how hard you try, they are never fully satisfied with your service? They just might not be a good fit for your business. Or you took them in when you knew you shouldn't have just because you thought could help them. If you happen to get one of these, maybe it's time to refer them to another company that can take better care of their needs. They might be much happier at another company. Are your marketing efforts not targeted and you are attracting too many of the wrong prospects? Time to review or revisit Week 5 - Target Marketing.9

Why do we put up with the bad customers anyway? Most of us are not anxious to lose business, especially when we are first starting out. We just want business no matter what. So, we just keep accepting the bad behavior or trying too hard with the wrong clientele.

Now is the time to change this and fire that customer that has been a pain in your side for too long!

Some ideas on how to dismiss the unwanted client:

- Write a letter (great article about how to write a dismissal letter: https://bit.ly/2OOo8XA).
- Staff training on what and how to inform the customer they are no longer welcome the next time they come to your business or call in.
- If the customer insists on coming to you, charge them a higher rate for your services. I know of several business owners who do this and are less aggravated to deal with them for a price.

- Simply inform the customer that you can no longer per-form the services for them and refer them to another business that you feel can take better care of them.

Your assignment this week:

- Make a list of those clients you no longer want to work with
- Seek a list from your team.
- Choose a process to dismiss them. You may use different processes with different customers.
- If you work with clients on an annual basis, such as tax preparation, schedule to dismiss these in a timely manner so they have time to find another provider.

Review this procedure on an annual basis, or on an as-needed basis. You and your team will be so much happier.

Next week we talk more about your favorite subject—you!

CHAPTER 50

WEEK 49—FIND A REPLACEMENT

———

"My mentor told me on my first day on the job as President of the Board that I should start looking for my replacement."

—TERRY HARPER, *PAST EXECUTIVE DIRECTOR,*

US SYNCHRONIZED SWIMMING

My wife is the Head of the Health Services Department for The Harker School. The school is a very large private school in San Jose. She oversees three nurses on three different campuses and 5 substitute nurses she utilizes on a regular basis. She oversees the entire staff of the school to get regular CPR and First Aid training and certification. Her role includes keeping health records of every student, interacting with and giving out health alerts to the faculty and the parents of the students whenever there is a crisis, such as outbreaks of infectious diseases or possible excessive smoke inhalation due to forest fires. She has quite a role to fill and difficult for anyone else to take over on short notice.

She has been on the job for over thirty years and is looking to retire in the next few years. Looking for a replacement is something she started to do recently. As someone who takes responsibility for her job, she has taken it upon herself to make sure her eventual replacement will be trained and ready the day she does retire. Part of this includes making sure all her duties and roles are well documented. In the process of hiring nurses, she has been looking for the person who can fill that role and not the other way around. (Hiring hint: always hire a person that fits the role, do not adapt a role to fit a person.) It is a big job and she wants to make sure she leaves it in good hands. After all, she was the very first school nurse they ever had, and she is the person who developed the whole program.

WHAT ABOUT REPLACING YOU?

How does this apply to you? Do you have a plan to replace you? There are many reasons why you should consider finding your replacement:

- You want to expand the business to many more locations—you need to have one of you in every location.
- You want to work less hours in the business and more on and have the ability to take more time off.
- You want to grow the scope and size of your current business. You will take on a more specific role and more of what you do now would be parsed out to many others.
- You plan to sell your business to an existing employee (current or future) or family.
- You plan to sell your business to someone who will retain the legacy of high-quality service and/or products your customers are accustomed to. And you hope to secure the ongoing employment of your team.
- You want someone trained well enough to replace you if something tragic were to happen to you.

You do have other options other than replacing yourself: you just sell the business to somebody and walk away. Or just close your doors when you want to retire or move on to something else. But there is a possibility you might get more money for the business if you sell it to an existing employee who knows they can walk into a business they already know and is profitable.

STEPS TO FINDING A REPLACEMENT:

- Have your own job and duties description completed. (See Week 12 - What's Your Role).
- List the desirable traits and qualities you feel your replacement should have. This exercise works for the other positions in your company as well.
- Look at your current staff members or your family members that might meet your criteria for replacing you.
- Set a timeline for your exit and begin the process of training your replacement.

You may find what you think is a great candidate, but in the end, they disqualify themselves. Been there, done that myself. Another piece of advice: No else is like you. Your candidate will think differently. What you are looking for is someone with similar ideals and qualities, but they may not do the job exactly as you would.

DO YOU LEAD AN ORGANIZATION?

I learned the lesson of looking for my replacement during my time as a youth leader. I learned the concept from the leader of our group as one of his officers. Early on, he tapped me to be his replacement at the end of his term of office. We spent a lot of time together that year with him mentoring me on everything the job entailed. The following year, I did the same with one of my officers. I have followed this practice in every leadership position I have held in the many nonprofits I have worked with.

How about you? If you have followed the advice of the chapters on joining organizations, you are, or soon will be, on a board and/or have a leadership position. You owe it to yourself, to the organization, and to your successor to start looking for your replacement the day you take office. If you don't, you may be there for too long (if there are no term limits) or create some challenges for the organization if you don't help them find a replacement.

Your assignment this week:

- Determine when your current role/position will change (retirement, sale of business, expansion, end of term, etc.).
- Determine the qualifications required of the role.
- Start looking for a qualified individual and start the mentoring process.
- This is not an annual assignment like many others, but something that you may revisit as things change in your business and your life.

You owe this to your clientele, employees, your family, and your community to find your replacement.

Just a few weeks left of this book! Next up: time for some business analysis.

CHAPTER 51

WEEK 50—S.W.O.T.

———

"War is 90 percent information. "

— NAPOLEON BONAPARTE

In business, as in war, having the right information is the key to survival. This is where a good SWOT analysis comes in.

Several years ago my wife volunteered to be a chaperone for a business club/class competition to be attended by some students of the school she works for as their school nurse. The organization is called DECA. It started many years ago to teach high school students all about business and marketing concepts and the many other fields related to those concepts. After her first weekend of chaperoning, she told me that I would really enjoy the program and encouraged me to volunteer. I did so, and as my wife stated, have enjoyed it immensely on many levels: to help coach the students on their presentations, judge the many events, listen to some very intelligent students present some amazing business plans, and I learned a lot from them. One of the things I learned more about was SWOT.

A HELPFUL TOOL

I had heard of the term *"SWOT Analysis"* many years before, but never paid it much attention. Based on my own (mis) understanding, I thought it was a big company strategy and that it was not applicable to myself or those businesses I was working with. But today, I consider it a helpful tool in reviewing and growing one's business, no matter what size.

A good SWOT analysis can assist a business owner in taking a good look at where they are now, where they might be in the future and how they may need to make changes to their current plans to address any potential changes on the horizon. The results of this exercise can have an effect on many areas of your business, especially in relation to your marketing, your target market, and maybe even the core of what you are currently doing.

Unless you have jumped from the start of this book to this chapter, you have done many different exercises over that last many months that should make you more able to understand this tool and to answer the questions to complete the analysis.

Here is an infographic that will help to familiarize yourself with S.W.O.T.:

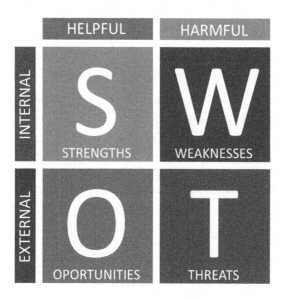

Here is a sample analysis for a florist:

- Strengths—What do you do very well?
    - Many repeat customers who come to us for business
    - Many online referrals from review websites
    - We already offer unique, custom products
    - Event planners prefer to get packaged deals for discounts

- Weaknesses
  - Only four employees to handle increased business volume
  - Extra paperwork and record-keeping
  - Customers may be confused about our offerings
  - Must check with Doug about volume of chocolate orders for large-scale events
- Opportunities
  - No other florist offers custom chocolates
  - Great as an add-on order for busy customers
  - Online order capacity
  - Free co-branding of catalog and sales materials
- Threats:
  - Chocolate shortages from global weather events could cause trouble with supply
  - Pricing not a staple
  - People may go to grocery stores' floral departments for cheaper bulk orders of chocolate and flowers
  - There's a chocolatier opening down the street next month

There are many articles and samples online that can give you more education on performing a SWOT analysis. You can find some that are dedicated to specific industries. Feel free to search online for additional information prior to doing this week's assignment. Here are a couple of great links to visit and help in performing your own SWOT analysis:

https://bit.ly/2xn63Yr

https://bit.ly/2htRtEH

https://bit.ly/2MFhBM6

Your assignment this week:

- Perform a SWOT Analysis on your business—make a
  list in each area
  - Strengths
    - Your experience
    - Your competencies
    - Assets, location,
    - Your structure, procedures, operations
  - Weaknesses
    - What areas are you lacking (procedures, mar-
      keting, etc.
    - What can you do better?
    - What is costing you too much money (possible
      losses), cash flow issues?
    - Market saturation?
    - Resources?
  - Opportunities
    - Where are there new market potentials?
    - Any possible expansion of existing business?

- Any new needs/niches/economic changes to take advantage of?
    - Any changes to your community?
    - New technology to be taken advantage of?
  - Threats:
    - What potential negative economic changes?
    - What potential negative social/political trends?
    - New competition?
    - Any potential challenges to your physical location?
    - Any other vulnerabilities?

Many of these questions are similar in each of the other quadrants. You are just looking for answers to related to the appropriate heading.

You should repeat this exercise on an annual basis, or whenever you feel the need to, to make some changes in operations/marketing/expansion, etc. due to internal or external forces.

See you next week when we will seek something new.

CHAPTER 52

WEEK 51—CHANGE: BE DISRUPTIVE/ INNOVATIVE/ADD A NEW NICHE

"Learning and innovation go hand in hand. The arrogance of success is to think that what you did yesterday will be sufficient for tomorrow."

—WILLIAM POLLARD

The railroads in the United States had many years of great success. Starting in the 1840s and on into the 1920s they were the main mode of transportation and moving freight across the country. The rails opened the country as nothing else had done before. The rail lines were everywhere. The train was an important lifeline for supplies in the Civil War and the destruction of the rails in the South was one part of the winning strategy of the Union. Many of the wealthiest men in history were the owners of a rail line. Those were heady times indeed for the railroads. But what happened?

TECHNOLOGY CHANGES THE WORLD.

There were two new inventions that started affecting the railroads. Both would alter our world and affect the railways enormously—the auto and the airplane. (The airplane decimated the cruise ship business as well, until it reinvented itself!) With the advent of the auto and heavy trucks, the train started to fall out of favor in both passenger and freight hauling as early as the 1920s. The train is a more efficient way to travel, but not as quick or convenient as the car, truck, or plane. It can only go where the rails are and it is slower due to the many stops it makes when going from one place to another. I have read that the owners of the rails had the opportunity to invest in the other technologies (they had the money) but opted not to and stuck with their business model. Today the rail lines are a mere shadow of what they once were and are mostly dependent on government subsidies. If this were your business, what might you have done to adapt?

The railroads are just one of many that have been affected by technological changes. Can you think of the others? Here are a few that were very big in the last half of the 20th century, but almost non-existent (or gone entirely) in the 21st century:

- Electronic stores—Radio Shack, Circuit City, and TV repair shops
- Video Rentals—Hollywood Video, Blockbuster, privately owned shops
- Record Stores—Tower Records closed their last store in 2006
- Film cameras and film processing—Kodak (Digital cameras have taken a hit with the advent of the Smartphone)
- Typewriters—manufacturing, ink rolls, and repairs
- Phone booths—privatized in the 70s and now all gone

ADAPT OR CHANGE OR?

No matter what business you are in, changes in technology and society can have a good or bad effect on your business. If you have followed this book week by week, you will have completed the previous chapter and done your SWOT analysis. What weaknesses and/or opportunities did you discover? Did you find that you need to add a new line of business to supplant or replace your current mix of business? Or are you now looking to grow in an entirely new direction? Or maybe your marketing is the only thing you need to adjust—change the message to change the perception of your business. An example of changing your message would be to promote your company as a *"Green business,"* something unheard of many years ago.

Changes in technology or society should be looked upon as opportunities to expand or jump into new areas of your industry that others might shy away from. So many people operate out of fear of change and the unknown that they stick with what they know only to find themselves left behind and eventually out of business. But that's not you.

SERVICES ARE NOT IMMUNE

Service businesses would seem immune to the many changes but look at how people shop for and pay for the services they use. If you run a service business and are not up on all the technology needed to remain competitive (web presence, payment options, the tools you use, etc.) you will be left behind by those embracing today's technology. There are many new web-based programs such as TaskRabbit that are affecting many businesses.

What if you embraced the new technology and made that a whole new line of business? I remember when digital cameras had just come out. I was working with a sign and graphics company that was the first in the area to use digital photography. They would Photoshop the new proposed signs into the picture and were able to show the client what it would look like before the sign was even made! They got very busy. Yes, others eventually caught on, but the business had a head start with a reputation for being very adaptive and creative while everyone else was playing catch up.

WHAT TO DO?

Maybe you are already up to date with all the changes happening, but you have reached the limits of your facility and can't seem to make any more money. Expanding to another location may be one option. But what else could you do? What if you came up with a sideline product or service that is a natural fit with your current business? Or eliminate one product or service that is no longer that profitable and add a new one that is on the cutting edge (like the digital photo idea) and be the first in your area to offer it? Time to think outside of the box. Here are some ideas that others have used:

- Sell your products online.
- Add a new line of services or products that compliment your current business. A few examples:
  - Restaurant—sell take out, sell your specialty food in the local markets, do catering, brew your own beer, offer cooking classes off hours or off site

- Printer—sell promotional items, graphics services, vehicle wraps, offer classes on using software programs
- Manufacturing—create and sell items made up of scrap materials (A local tire store chain sells furniture made from old tires)
- Construction/remodeling—offer interior design consulting, house cleaning, niche construction (e.g. wine cellars)
- Computer sales and repairs—networking support, classes on anything computer related
- Offer something radically different than your competitors
  - An outrageous warranty
  - Extended or unusual hours that others don't offer
  - Concierge level service—standout as an exclusive business
  - A new service that no one else offers (Amazon did this, maybe you can too.)

The whole point of this exercise is to find other ways to enhance or adapt your business to the coming changes or one up the competition by doing something very differently without affecting your core business.

Your assignment this week:

- Review your SWOT results to see where Weaknesses and Opportunities are.
- Determine what you can do differently or enhance what you are doing now.
- What new sideline product or service can you add that compliments what you are doing now?
- Implement your idea—this might not happen this week, but you can get started on it.

Change is the one constant of the universe. Those, like you, who are ready for it and embrace it will not only survive but thrive.

See you next week as we begin to wrap up this year together

CHAPTER 53

IT HAS BEEN A YEAR ALREADY—NOW WHAT?

Congratulations! If you are reading this, you should have made it through all the chapters by now. And having just returned from your vacation, you should be well rested and wondering what to do next. Let's discuss what you can do to get more from this book and review what you have accomplished this year:

#1—Keep having your weekly appointment with yourself. It should be an ingrained habit by now and it will be hard to break, unless you revert to your old ways of reacting to the Urgent Unimportant things that can come up at any time. You have a great habit, so keep it up!

#2—Start the book all over again. It was designed to be used over and over, year after year. (Eventually you will have to buy the Revised Edition). You may find that:

- there are other aspects of a topic to explore and expand on
- you have learned more and want to refine last year's efforts
- there is a need to review an area annually (such as vendors, HR issues, etc.) as noted in the text
- you have some of the assignments still in progress and need to do more work on them
- as you re-read a chapter you will discover something new

#3—You may find yourself fully satisfied with some chapters and want to substitute them for other areas that can improve your business. If you go to my website www.1week1thing.com, you will find:

- a list of other topics that you can work on instead
- enhancements to the existing chapters
- updates and more stories and more links

"No book or poem is ever finished, merely abandoned."

—HYPERION, DAN SIMMONS

Just like the quote above, I found it challenging to stop writing because I wanted things to be perfect for you, the reader, and to give you a lot more information. It is kind of like gardening: You keep planting because you are so looking forward to eating all that bounty of your work. But you are out of room to plant and you will never be able to eat all that you harvest, not to mention the amount of time it takes to tend to all those plants. I did not want to stuff you with too much information at one time.

No business is ever finished either. There is always something more to do, to improve upon, and to grow. This book was designed to accompany you in that process.

Several of the contributors to this book have been giving me some great feedback for more stories to share and even other book ideas to build on this one. One suggestion from an ecstatic contributor is a book focused on the solopreneur (the business with no employees). Stay tuned.

If you have not already done so, please sign up for my weekly blog and follow me on all my social media pages and like any of my posts. (Remember what I said about getting online in the chapter on web presence?) You can send me an email at jeff@1week1thing.com if you have a question, suggestion, or if you are looking for coaching or a speaker to present to your group or association. I appreciate you sharing your journey and stories about how this book has helped you in any way. And the others in this community will appreciate those stories, as well.

The Japanese have a word for constant and never-ending improvement: Kaisen. In the book *Raving Fans* by Ken Blanchard and Sheldon Bowles, the third of the three ways to creating *"Raving Fans"* is to do 1 percent more. This book is designed to get you at least 1 percent better in all the areas covered in these pages. If that is all you accomplished each week, but I suspect more, you will have improved your business by 52 percent overall. Not a bad return on your investment of the purchase of this book and working two to three hours in 1 Week on 1 Thing.

I will close this book with my favorite personal quote:

"The difference between success and failure are quite small. It is the little things you do, or don't do, that make the difference."

CHAPTER 54T

WEEK 52—MILESTONES

———

"Book your next vacation as soon as possible after you get back from your last vacation."

—JIM FARRELL

I met Jim Farrell of Facilities First at a local networking event. He was an affable fellow and we established a good rapport from the first moment we met. He told me one thing that I have remembered more than almost any other statement in meeting thousands of people: the quote that opens this chapter.

His idea was profound. How many of us talk about taking a vacation or trip, but never get around to taking it? We delay with excuses like *"I don't have the time."* *"I just can't leave the business right now." "I don't have the money."* In the end, we may never go and live with regret for not going. His idea was to book your next trip a year in advance, pay the deposit and start planning how to make it happen. With that obligation made, you will work harder to make it happen than just hoping to take that vacation *"sometime this year"*. Now that is some great goal setting.

THE LAST ASSIGNMENT?

If you take Jim's advice, this is not only the last assignment in this book—it is the first one and the last one! Think of having the time off already booked as you start this book. How would that motivate you, knowing you have that trip (or just time off from the business) you have been meaning to take for some time? With the obligation made, your brain will work harder to make sure it will happen. There is a saying, *"We get what we seek,"* and another, *"We draw to ourselves what we focus on."*

Imagine having the tickets or the travel brochure hanging in your office. When you are having a tough week, but you see those tickets, you will be re-motivated to work through that week. It will energize you knowing that the prize of working to improve your business this year awaits you.

Where will you go? As you ask yourself this question, can you feel the excitement build just thinking of the places you might go? But you might be starting to make excuses about why you can't go: the cost, the time away from the business, and more. Excuses! Fear will show its face, as well. You might be asking yourself, *"What if I fail and I don't get business the way I want it and can't afford the trip?"* Now is the time to draw a line in the sand, face the fear, ditch the excuses, and make the commitment. You bought this book to build a better business. If you implement just several small portions of this book, you will have improved your business so much that you will be able to take that trip quite easily. You deserve it!

With so much success that you should be enjoying now and in the next year, you should book a two-week vacation. Even better, add an extended weekend away in the next 6 months. Again, you will have earned it.

SPECIAL NOTE

Not everyone will finish this book in one year. Some of you will be done early (you overachiever!). Or you could be someone that is taking a bit more time on each chapter and won't finish in a year. That's OK. Either way, you should take the time off and celebrate—you've earned it.

Your assignment this week:

- Take that trip.
- Ignore the business while you are away this week.
- Book the next trip the day after you get back (part of next week's assignment if you follow the last chapter's advice—read on).

Tag me in a picture of you on your trip on Facebook and/or Instagram. I look forward to seeing your smiling face.

ACKNOWLEDGEMENTS

This book may have come to me through divine inspiration, but it would not have come to be if were not for being in the right place at the right time (the universe doing its work) and for the help and support of many people. As I write these words, I still find it hard to believe that I have come so far in the completion of this book.

First, and most importantly, I thank my loving and ever so patient wife who has had many weekends alone while I was locked away in my office writing this book and for her reviews of most it, as well.

Secondly, I thank my family for supporting me and listening to the endless stories of my writing travails and my struggle to get those last few chapters completed.

Next, I want to thank the many who have contributed to the funding of the book (those that bought more than one has the number next to their name), gave me the time to interview them, and/or reviewed some of the first manuscript (noted by the asterisk). Special acknowledgement to Juliette Donohue who afforded some great feedback on a good portion of the titles, organization of the chapters and so much more.

Albert Cheknov	Andrea Nott*
Anna Koslova	Antra Getzhoff
Betty Kaufman	Bill Nott 10
Bob Melrose*	Brian Eaton
Cleve Dayton	Cody A. Crawford
Curt Conyers	Darren Penfield
David Bartosik	David Parker
Dawn Suiter	Donald Chu
Donnie Gupton	Doris Pickering
Eamon Rooney*	Elie Massabki

Elizabeth Ricktor

Gregg Fiscalini*

Henry Lonsdale 5

Joe Monte*

Juston Glass

Keith Baker*

Khadija Zanotto

Lauren Gardner

Loren Zemenick

Mark Gunnerson*

Maylan Newton*5

Mike Rosen 5

Peter Jones

Rebecca Wang

Gavin Lawrence

Griffin Germond

Jeff Meyers 2

Juliette Donohue* 10

Kathryn Oldershaw

Ken Shrum

Larry Moore*

Lee Lonitz*

Louis Bateh

Mary McClelland 2

Michelle Costanza

Nick Nikbaht

Ravinder Lal*

Richard Loek

Robert Crull   Sean Brand*

Shane Jacksteit*   Susan Nichol

Tammy Portoff   Thomas Broxholm

Tony Gordon

Another group I wish to thank is my fellow students in the book writing classes who were part of this endeavor and who contributed in their own ways. A special shout out to Karen Cornwell who introduced me to the class and without her invitation to join the group, this book might still be only in my journal.

And lastly, I wish to thank Eric Koester and all those at New Degree Press who have helped me along the way. Not only did they help with the development of this book and just how best to write it but were great encouragers along the way. These folks would be Brian Bies (who was especially patient with me), Jennifer Kennedy, Bailee Tracy, Amanda Brown, Ashley Goodnow, Chanda Elaine, Gjorgji Pejkovski, Leila Summers and Chau Le.

There were so many that contributed along the way that several of those may not have made this list. If you are one of those, I extend my thanks and appreciation for your support.

WORKS REFERENCED

———

INTRODUCTION

Covey, Stephen R. 1989. *The 7 Habits of Highly Effective People.* 1st ed. New York: Simon & Schuster.

Gerber, Michael E. 1995. *The E-Myth Revisited.* 3rd ed. New York: HarperCollins Books.

Small Business Administration. 2019. *"2019 Small Business Profile".* Washington D.C.: SBA. https://cdn.advocacy.sba.gov/wp-content/uploads/2019/04/23142719/2019-Small-Business-Profiles-US.pdf

https://www.sba.gov/sites/default/files/Business-Survival.pdf

https://www.ssa.gov/OACT/COLA/central.html

https://www.payscale.com/research/US/Job=Small_
Business_Owner_%2F_Operator/Salary/54db1997/
Self-Employed

HOW TO USE THIS BOOK

Covey, Stephen R., A. Roger Merrill, and Rebecca R. Merrill.
1994. *First Things First*. 1st ed. New York: Simon & Schuster.

WEEK 1

Hsieh, Tony. 2010. *Delivering Happiness*. 1st ed. New York:
Hachette Book Group.

Collins, Jim. 2019. *Good to Great* - Concepts https://www.
jimcollins.com/concepts/the-hedgehog-concept.html

WEEK 2

Juma, Aly. 2019. *"The 13 Virtues of Life: Benjamin Franklin's
Guide To Building Character"*. Blog. Alyjuma.Com. https://
alyjuma.com/13-virtues/.

Keller, Gary, and Jay Papasan. 2013. *The ONE Thing: The Surprisingly Simple Truth Behind Extraordinary Results*. 1st ed. Rellek Publishing Partners, Ltd.

Galla, Brain. 2018. *Why Willpower Is Overrated*. Blog. Vox. https://www.vox.com/science-and-health/2018/1/15/16863374/willpower-overrated-self-control-psychology

WEEK 3

Covey, Stephen R. 1989. *The 7 Habits of Highly Effective People*. 1st ed. New York: Simon & Schuster.

WEEK 3

RPNA Law Group. New California Sexual Harassment Training Requirements 2019, Blog http://rpnalaw.com/2019/02/08/new-california-sexual-harassment-training-requirements-2019/

WEEK 11

Rosebaum, Mike. 2018. Men's Long Jump World Records Blog. Liveaboutdotcom. https://www.liveabout.com/mens-long-jump-world-records-3258952

https://iri-training.com/coaching-statistics-value-coaching/

"*Restaurant Impossible*". 2019. TV program. Food Network.

WEEK 13

Mezger, Roger. 2019. Milk is no Cash Cow for Grocery Stores. Https://Www.Cleveland.Com/. https://www.cleveland.com/business/2008/08/milk_is_no_cash_cow_for_grocer.html

http://www.yourarticlelibrary.com/products/classification-of-buying-motives-product-buying-and-patronage-buying/22154

WEEK 14

https://en.wikipedia.org/wiki/Five_whys

WEEK 17

Beckwith, Harry. 1997. *Selling The Invisible*. 1st ed. New York: Warner Books, Inc.

WEEK 20

Kent, Germany. 2019. *"Goodreads"*. Www.Goodreads. Com. Accessed October 15. *https://www.goodreads.com/quotes/8414953-5-ways-to-build-your-brand-on-social-media-1*

Mendenhall, Nathan. 2019. *"A Data-Driven Look At What Consumers Want From Brands On Social Media"*. Blog. Social Media Today. *https://www.socialmediatoday.com/marketing/data-driven-look-what-consumers-want-brands-social-media*

WEEK 22

Photiades, Melissa. 2014. 6 Eye-Opening Employee Engagement Statistics

https://talentculture.com/6-eye-opening-employee-engagement-statistics/

WEEK 26

Collins, Jim. 2011. *Good To Great*. 3rd ed. New York: HarperCollins. https://paulminors.com/blog/good-to-great-jim-collins-book-summary-pdf/

Collins, Jim. 2011. *Good To Great*. 3rd ed. New York: HarperCollins. https://paulminors.com/blog/good-to-great-jim-collins-book-summary-pdf/

Dishman, Lydia. 2016 These are the best employee benefits https://www.fastcompany.com/3056205/these-are-the-best-employee-benefits-and-perks

Team, Glassdoor. 2019. *"Top 20 Employee Benefits & Perks For 2017"*.

Blog. Www.Glassdoor.Com/Blog. https://www.glassdoor.com/blog/top-20-employee-benefits-perks-for-2017/

"Biotech, Pharmaceutical and Clinical Research Jobs | Bio-Space". 2018. Www.Biospace.Com. *https://www.biospace.com/article/what-s-more-important-at-work-better-perks-and-benefits-or-a-higher-salary-/*

Pizzaro, Sal. 2019. Original Joe's closing for lunch? Say it ain't so! https://www.mercurynews.com/2019/02/01/original-joes-closing-for-lunch-say-it-aint-so/

WEEK 45

Sivers, Derek. 2011. *Anything You Want - 40 Lessons for A New Kind Of Entrepreneur.* 1st ed. Brilliance Audio, Inc.

WEEK 46

Barker, Eric. n.d. *Barking Up the Wrong Tree.* 1st ed. New York: Harper One.

WEEK 47

Clason, George S. 1988. *The Richest Man in Babylon.* New York: Signet Publishing

WEEK 48

Duran, Steven. 2016. How Southwest Lost A Customer. Medium.Com.

https://medium.com/@stevenduran_96808/a-story-about-how-southwest-airlines-lost-a-customer-5e6608b227fb

Kjerulf, Alexander. 2014. Top 5 Reasons Why 'The Customer Is Always Right' Is Wrong. https://www.huffpost.com/entry/top-5-reasons-customer-service_b_5145636

"*Railroad History*". 2019. American-Rails.Com. https://www. american-rails.com/history.html

IT'S BEEN A YEAR ALREADY. NOW WHAT?

Blanchard, Ken, and Sheldon Bowles. 1993. *Raving Fans.* New York: William Morrow and Company, Inc.

SUGGESTED
READING LIST

———

Here is my Suggested Reading list for you to start with. There are so many more good books to read. You can find many more suggestions online by topic or author. You have a few optional versions to read books: paper (my preference), audio (2nd favorite) or e-reader. But whatever way you choose, a good goal would be to read at least 1 book a month. Put it in your Default Calendar. You will be richly rewarded.

If you really want to get more out of what you read join a book club or challenge a friend or mentor to read the same books and meet to debrief each other weekly. Taking notes in a journal really helps, as well.

Another tip: you should vary your reading topics. Don't just read books on business. I suggest you read more about people and what makes them tick. You will more about yourself in doing so.

Selling The Invisible – Harry Beckwith*

Raving Fans – Ken Blanchard*

The E-Myth Revisited – Michael Gerber

The 7 Habits of Highly Successful People – Stephen Covey*

To Sell is Human – Daniel Pink

Barking up the Wrong Tree – Eric Barker

The Game of Work – Charles Coonradt*

The Better People Leader - Charles Coonradt

Spin Selling – Neil Rackman

Now Discover Your Strengths – Clifton Fadiman*

The Magic of Thinking Big – David Schwartz

How to Win Friends and Influence People – Dale Carnegie

All In – Adrian Gostick and Chester Elton

The One Minute Manager – Ken Blanchard*

Extreme Ownership – Jaco Willink & Leif Babin

The One Thing – Gary Keller

The Purple Cow – Seth Godin*

Made to Stick – Chip & Dan Heath*

Little Red Book of Selling – Jeffrey Gitomer*

Crucial Conversations – Patterson, Grenny, McMillan & Switzler *

The Small Big – Martin, Goldstein & Cialdini

*These are some of my favorite authors and suggest you read many of their books.